WILTSHIRE'S HAUNTED PUBS & INNS

But, soft: behold! lo where it comes again!
I'll cross it, though it blast me. — Stay, illusion!
If thou hast any sound, or use a voice.
Speak to me.

William Shakespeare: *Hamlet*, I.I

we hope you can
visit some of these!
Happy Birthday
from Sue + Larry

First published in Great Britain in 2019

Copyright © Terry Townsend 2019

British Library Cataloguing-in-Publication Data
A CIP record for this title is available from the
British Library

ISBN 978 0 85710 122 8

PiXZ Books
Halsgrove House, Ryelands Business Park,
Bagley Road, Wellington, Somerset TA21 9PZ
Tel: 01823 653777
Fax: 01823 216796
email: sales@halsgrove.com

An imprint of Halstar Ltd, part of the
Halsgrove group of companies
Information on all Halsgrove titles is
available at: www.halsgrove.com

Printed and bound in India by
Parksons Graphics

Wiltshire's HAUNTED PUBS & INNS

Terry Townsend

To my wife Carol

with thanks for her continued
patience, indispensable help and support

CONTENTS

TERRY TOWNSEND'S OTHER
HALSGROVE TITLES INCLUDE:

*Once Upon a Pint – A Readers' Guide to the
Literary Pubs & Inns of Dorset & Somerset*

*Dorset Smugglers' Pubs
More Dorset Smugglers' Pubs
East Cornwall Smugglers' Pubs: Kingsand to Mevagissey
East Devon Smugglers' Pubs
East Sussex Smugglers' Pub
Hampshire Smugglers' Pubs,
Isle of Wight Smugglers' Pubs,
Kent Smugglers' Pubs,
Suffolk Smugglers' Pubs
West Cornwall Smugglers' Pubs: St Ives to Falmouth*

Bristol & Clifton Slave Trade Trails

*Jane Austen & Bath
Jane Austen's Hampshire
Jane Austen's Kent*

ACKNOWLEDGEMENTS

My thanks go to the following:
Brenda Stables for her proof reading help;
Karen Binaccioni for her expert contribution with layout and design;
Debora Clogg, volunteer at Malmesbury Museum, for sharing her knowledge of the town and its spooky pubs.

I would also like to extend a big thank you to all the pub licensees plus their staff and customers who took the time to tell me of their own paranormal experiences.

Former agitated spirits at The Bridge Inn, Horton; The Crown at Pewsey and The Jolly Tar at Hannington now seem to have settled down.

Location Map

CASTLE EATON •

• MALMESBURY

WANBOROUGH •

• Chippenham

CORSHAM •

• AVEBURY

MONKTON
FARLEIGH •

• BECKHAMPTON

BRADFORD-
ON-AVON •

• Melksham

• AVONCLIFF

• Devizes

W i l t s h i r e

• CORSLEY HEATH

Amesbury •

Salisbury •

• DOWNTON

Introduction

Andrew Swift and Kirsten Elliott in *The Inns of Wiltshire* say:

'To know Wiltshire's inns is to know Wiltshire'. The history of the county's inns has been inextricably linked to the lives of ordinary – and extraordinary – people for countless generations'.

This is undoubtedly true but there is another Wiltshire which may well be unknowable. A county of crop circles, UFO sightings and hauntings. This weird alternative Wiltshire has an unexplained magnetic energy. A force so powerfully compelling to Neolithic and Bronze Age Britons they were inspired to drag stones weighing up to 80 tons each, across 167 miles of arduous open country in order to erect the world's most famous and puzzling monument. This magnetism continues to exude its power today. More than one and a half million people visited Stonehenge last year to simply stand and wonder.

The summer solstice at Stonehenge. More than one and a half million people visited the site last year to simply stand and wonder.

The county is full of traces of prehistoric people and has more visible ancient sites than any other. Among these relics are the numerous 'long barrow' burial mounds and one man who has made a career of exploring these secret places is Phil Harding, Wessex Archaeologist, Salisbury resident and regular face on Channel 4's *TimeTeam*. In a forward to *Haunted Salisbury* by Frogg Moody and Richard Nash' Phil said:

> *'Ever since our ancient ancestors confined their dead to the afterlife, the spirit world has proved to be a potent influence to people across the world; and still is, despite increased secular attitudes in modern society. Some souls have proved to be more restless than others and have refused to lie down'.*

This reluctance of some souls to lie down seems to manifest particularly in pubs. Over the years my interest in social history has led me to write extensively about this most enduring of English institutions. I have explored smugglers' pubs throughout the southern maritime counties from Cornwall to Kent and even up into East Anglia. In writing topographical books tracing Jane Austen's life, I visited numerous coaching inns across three counties. Researching the Bristol slave trade I discovered a dozen or more old taverns inextricably involved with that shameful traffic. What I found repeatedly, when discussing the history of a particular pub with staff and customers, someone would invariably say... *and there is a ghost*!

When my publisher first suggested I write a book about haunted pubs and inns, I took a while to consider the proposal because I wasn't personally convinced such things existed. He pointed out that ghost stories endure in abundance and some of them are the most captivating tales ever told. After some consideration I realised few people have failed to meet someone who has not encountered an apparition or inexplicable presence within a room. When I consented to explore the phenomenon of haunted hostelries, Wiltshire seemed to be the obvious place to start.

The Moody and Nash book, mentioned previously, features

three Salisbury pubs: the Haunch of Venison – the city's most haunted pub, The Rai d'Or – which in a former life was a medieval brothel and The City Lodge nowadays providing only accommodation, but was formerly The Catherine Wheel public house. Here, at the time of the Civil War, a Cavalier officer was reputedly catapulted out through a window, as if by an explosion, when drunkenly cursing and denouncing the devil.

Remaining sceptical but undoubtedly intrigued I was eager to explore the city's ancient drinking dens. My initial Salisbury safari provided the opportunity to add the splendid Red Lion. I even discovered The Blue Boar Tudor tavern, located in the basement of Debenhams department store. Naturally I couldn't stop there; presented with the promise of a window on Wiltshire's other world, a realm where things go bump in the night and empty rooms echo with the sound of weeping, where corridors reverberate with the thump of heavy footsteps and inanimate objects can fly. However, it took me a while to discover the glass in this window is opaque.

A Window on Wiltshire's Other World

The next step on my paranormal pub crawl was Amesbury where enquiries led me to the genteel Agatha Christie style Antrobus Hotel where The Beatles stayed in 1965 when filming *HELP!* on nearby Salisbury Plain. It was here I learned hotels and inns are not necessarily shy about promoting their ghostly heritage, or even reticent about identifying their most haunted rooms. It seems guests relishing the potential opportunities of experiencing spine tingling 'other worldly' happenings, outnumber those who might be frightened off by tales of the unexpected. This was also the first of a number of establishments I visited who actually organise popular 'ghost hunting' evenings. Indeed, most of the pubs and inns I feature in this book have at one time invited paranormal investigators to conduct surveys.

I also happened on a further consideration for those in pursuit of the paranormal: the emerging opportunity provided by Closed Circuit Television (CCTV). A bizarre incident was picked up by the security cameras at The Antrobus, which you can watch on YouTube and make up your own mind. Members of a paranormal investigatory team are seen quietly taking tea in the bar when an inanimate decorative lantern on the counter behaves in the most extraordinary way.

A decorative lantern of the type seen behaving bizarrely on YouTube was caught on CCTV at The Antrobus Hotel, Amesbury.

From Amesbury I moved on to Avebury and The Red Lion in its unique location at the centre of the largest prehistoric stone circle in the world. This certainly appears to be one of the places where the spirits refuse to lie down. It is the largest stone circle in Britain – originally consisting of about 100 stones – which in turn encloses two smaller stone circles. At the centre of this vast sacred land-scape is Avebury Village and its haunted pub.

Here, in the friendly bar, I chatted with staff and locals who were confirmed in their belief of supernatural happenings. They conveyed a quiet confidence, unimpressed by what they judged to be the histrionics of Yvette Fielding, presenter of

The Red Lion at Avebury stands at the centre of the world's largest stone circle.

the TV show *Most Haunted*. So spooked was Yvette during her visit she fled vowing never to return. A cartoon of her in the dining room says it all.

It was at The Red Lion I first encountered the willingness of people to relate their personal stories of paranormal experiences. The enthusiasm I met with became a pattern repeated across the county and the readiness to talk was equally true for people in popular pubs or high class hotels. I spoke to individuals from all walks of life, men and women from young bar staff, to customers of retirement age. Some were initially a little hesitant but soon warmed to the subject. It's an accepted fact people tend to exaggerate things they think are likely to enhance their self-image. Men might boast of sexual conquests or the size of a fish that got away. Some women are happy to embellish stories of their children's success. However, to claim to have seen a ghost does not really further anybody's status or reputation.

Regulars at Avebury's famously haunted Red Lion were unimpressed by Yvette Fielding's histrionics when she fled from the pub.

The question I kept asking myself was this: if these stories are just fantasy why were people repeating them? Many of the tales I heard were expressed with passion and often in considerable detail. You may think, as I was chatting to people in pubs, alcohol was the influencing factor; indeed that all sightings of pub ghosts can be ascribed to alcohol-induced hallucinations but you'd be wrong. It is true some of the customers I spoke to were enjoying a drink but they were not drunk and the management and staff were strictly sober. I concluded my interviewees' experiences were genuine to them and they were among the alliance of people who are more sensitive and receptive to things ethereal.

The other factor I discovered was wherever I travelled in Wiltshire I was never far from a haunted pub. Throughout the

county, the procession of phantom monks, Cavaliers and veiled ladies wafts in and out of our familiar dimension. In remote rural inns and busy urban ones alike, footsteps are heard on staircases and along empty corridors. Doors open and close on their own, taps and lights go on and off, temperatures drop suddenly and inexplicably, electrical appliances behave very oddly, things fall off walls and shelves, staff and customers are nudged by invisible entities and sleepers woken by unidentified bedroom intruders.

Sleeping Spirits

Ghosts it seems do not like change. Poltergeist activity often occurs when new people take over or there are structural alterations to a building. The reported phenomenon of ghosts walking through walls might be attributed to the fact the wall simply wasn't there when the person departed this life. Their spectre continues to follow the established routes they knew before their transition to the spirit world. A change in original floor levels might also explain levitation sightings.

Following up on reports of historical hauntings, I visited pubs where former agitated spirits seemed to have settled down. Licensees at The Jolly Tar at Hannington, The Crown at Pewsey and The Bridge Inn at Horton for example suggested the original stories might be attributed to previous landlords with an eye to a publicity opportunity. However, Barry Leighton a reporter from the *Wiltshire News*, witnessed an antique pistol fall from a wall while he was interview-

Jim and Veronica Fay, former licensees of The Crown at Pewsey, with the antique pistol that flew from the wall while they were being interviewed by a photographer and reporter from the *Wiltshire News*.

ing Pewsey licensees Jim and Veronica Fay about a range of unexplained happenings at The Crown. The current landlord of The Bridge Inn at Horton is adamant his pub is no longer haunted; if it ever was. However, he did concede, during work to install a disabled toilet, a reportedly haunted bricked up vaulted chamber was revealed and some months later he began to fear the paint in this area would never dry.

A Lasting Legacy

Why is it so many pubs and inns are said to be haunted? I think the answer might lie in the word 'pub' itself. Other buildings like abbeys, castles and stately homes are often associated with supernatural happenings but they have an element of exclusivity compared with the local pub which is everybody's heritage. The intrinsic thing about a pub is that it is a 'public' house, where the doors are open every day to anyone who has the price of a drink.

Pubs have been an integral part of our social life for over a thousand years and, as Andrew Swift and Kirsten Elliott pointed out, have played a significant part in our country's

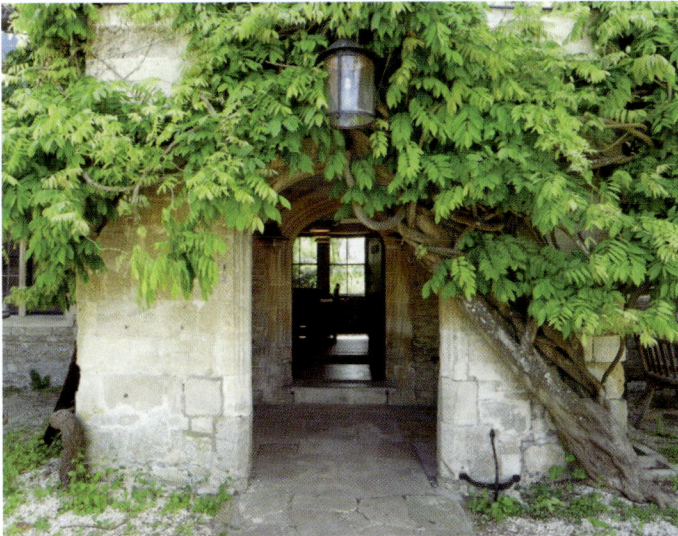

The monastic origins of The King's Arms at Monkton Farleigh are clear to see.

history. Through turbulent times and periods of peace they have provided a place for people of all social classes to meet and exchange news, to discuss problems, to conduct business and enjoy the company of friends.

From its beginnings in the monastic hospice, through the coaching age to the present day town or village local these institutions have offered hospitality to thousands of people over hundreds of years. They have played a considerable part in innumerable life stories and so it seems natural they should also feature prominently in many end of life stories. If walls could talk surely those of an English pub or inn would hold the monopoly on drama. In this context it seems unsurprising the words 'haunted pub' fit as naturally into our lexicon as 'ghost stories' fit into our folk heritage.

Salisbury resident Phil Harding who has a passion for ancient bones and locally brewed ale keeps an open mind on other worldly possibilities.

The hostelries I feature in this book represent a complete cross section from canal side taverns to ancient inns and even some that have evolved into restaurants and smart hotels. As you have read this far it seems likely you will visit at least some of them. I can't guarantee you will see a ghost but it's a fair bet you will meet some people who have, or will tell you they have. If you remain sceptical, it might be worth pondering on what British geneticist and evolutionary biologist J.B.S. Haldane is often quoted as saying,

'My own suspicion is that the universe is not only stranger than we suppose, but stranger than we can suppose.'

Amesbury
The Antrobus Hotel

15 Church Street, Amesbury SP4 7EU

Tel: 01980 623163

www.antrobushotel.co.uk

On Monday 16 July 2018 the *Daily Mail* reported on a paranormal incident that took place in the bar at The Antrobus Hotel while a trio from the ghost hunting team *Paranormal Wiltshire* were present. Selena Wright from Devizes, founder of the team, and her friend Karin Beasant were relaxing in the bar in the middle of the day enjoying a cup of tea and some biscuits when the bizarre episode occurred.

The moment was captured on the hotel's CCTV and can be viewed on YouTube. The door of a decorative lantern standing on the bar mysteriously flies open when there is no one anywhere near it. Selena said:

The former private house, prep school and vicarage finally became a hotel in 1923.

'We heard one hell of a loud clicking sound, which unfortunately wasn't caught on the CCTV, as the lantern door clicked we all immediately turned and looked at it. We sat there with our jaws wide open, thinking is this really happening?'

Ms Wright later used a spirit level to check the bar was

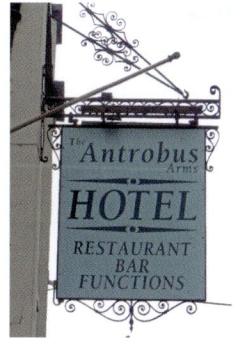

The later addition of this solid wall in the function room does not hinder the ghost of the white lady passing through the mirror.

completely flat. She also examined the catch on the lantern door which she found '*stiff to close*' and concluded: '*It's flummoxed us all*'.

General Manager of The Antrobus Hotel, Damian Kuczera said many former employees claim to have experienced unexplained events and sightings within the hotel and its grounds including apparitions and reports of items moving. He explained:

The bar counter on which the recent bizarre lantern door incident occurred.

*'The hotel has a rich, happy history and is well known by guests
and staff for strange occurrences, though none of them negative.
We were fascinated to have captured the lantern moment on
camera, but I don't think it comes as a surprise to many of our
staff or regulars.'*

A couple of guest rooms are particularly noted for unexplained happenings and a ghostly lady dressed in white has
been seen passing directly through the large mirror hanging
on the wall in the function room. Two phantom children aged
around six and seven are also seen in various locations and
are thought to be the ghosts of two youngsters who drowned
in a former pond at the far end of the garden when the building was a private house.

Two young chil-
dren were said to
have drowned in
the large pond
that existed many
years ago at the
far end of the
lawned garden
when the grounds
were part of
Wyndersham
House estate.

In 1635 four tenements and an inn The Chopping Knife occupied the present site. These were demolished in 1848 and
Wyndersham House was built in their place. In 1867 the

house was converted into a prep school for young gentlemen. In 1881 it became a vicarage and finally, in 1923, a hotel.

Much of the foundations are original and includes those of The Chopping Knife. Legend has it that within the hotel's expansive cellar network are several tunnels that once led off to the former abbey and other public houses. These subterranean passages would have originally been used by monks particularly during the period of Henry VIII's dissolution of the monasteries. The hotel holds regular overnight ghost hunting events.

The site of this former mediaeval well is located deep in the expansive cellar.

Amesbury
The George Hotel

High Street, Amesbury SP4 7ET

Tel: 01980 622108

www.relaxinnz.co.uk/amesbury

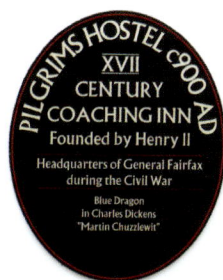

PILGRIMS HOSTEL c900 AD
XVII CENTURY COACHING INN
Founded by Henry II

Headquarters of General Fairfax
during the Civil War

Blue Dragon
in Charles Dickens
"Martin Chuzzlewit"

The first mention of The George as an inn was in 1490, although its foundations date back to c.900. Roundhead Commander, General Thomas Fairfax, used the inn as his headquarters during the English Civil War. Over the intervening years a succession of celebrated guests stopped here including a number of kings and famous writers. Charles Dickens used to stay when travelling to visit his parents in the West Country. Dickens established his debt prone father in a cottage near Exeter to detach him from temptations and opportunities afforded in London. The George is not however (as a plaque on the pub claims) The Blue Dragon of his novel *Martin Chuzzlewitt* which is described in the story as a small village alehouse some distance from the main coaching route.

The first mention of The George as an inn was in 1490, although its foundations date back to circa 900.

Visiting ghost hunters have noted the greatest concentration of paranormal activities around the area of the main staircase.

Parliamentary General Thomas Fairfax made his headquarters at The George Inn during the English Civil War.

With such an illustrious history it's not surprising the venerable old inn exhibits any number of manifestations. Visiting ghost hunters have noted the greatest concentration of paranormal activities around the area of the main staircase and along the corridor leading to room 6. Adults, young children and even a black cat have been seen.

The most consistent report is of a phantom soldier from the First World War dressed in the familiar khaki uniform and wrap around gaiters. When the Tommy manifests he is accompanied by the sound of horses trotting around the

Opposite page: Spirits of adults, young children and even a black cat have been seen or sensed along the corridor leading to room 6.

When the ghost of the First World War soldier is seen he is accompanied by the sound of horses trotting around the courtyard.

courtyard suggesting he could be one of the fallen listed on Amesbury's war memorial who in a former life took care of horses stabled at the inn.

Could it be that the First World War soldier formerly took care of horses stabled at the inn?

TO THE GLORY OF GOD AND IN EVERLASTING MEMORY OF THE AMESBURY MEN WHO GAVE THEIR LIVES IN THE GREAT WAR 1914 – 1918.

LT. EDMUND ANTROBUS
CAPT. TYRELL E. HOLLAND. M.C. CHR. LEGION D. HONNEUR
MAJOR GEN. FREDERICK D. V. WING C.B.

PTE. LEWIS W. ALDRIDGE	PTE. FRANK GOULD	PTE. HARRY O. SMITH
L'CPL. HENRY G. BARTHOLOMEW	PTE. CHARLES J. HIBBS	PTE. F. CHARLES SOUTHEY
PTE. E. GEORGE BATCHELOR	CPL. GEORGE HUNT	PTE. LEWIS V. SOUTHEY
PTE. WILFRED L. BUCKLAND	PTE. CHARLES W. LAWRENCE	PTE. FREDERICK J. STEVENS
PTE. FREDERICK R. CANNING	CPL. E. JAMES LAWRENCE	PTE. EDWIN TAVES
PTE. ALBERT E. CHAMBERS	PTE. PERCY NETTON	PTE. JOSEPH H. THORNE
STOKER GEORGE DOWNER	A.B. GEORGE PALMER	A.B. NORMAN H. VALLACE
PTE. CHARLES FORD	PTE. GEORGE W. PETHEN	PTE. WILLIAM J. WALLEN
PTE. GEORGE FORD	CPL. WALTER PIKE	A.B. ARTHUR F. WHATLEY
PTE. JAMES FORD		PTE. HECTOR G. WHITE

Three officers and twenty nine private soldiers from the small town of Amesbury sacrificed their lives in Flanders fields.

Avebury
The Red Lion

High Street, Avebury SN8 1RF

Tel: 01672 539266

www.greeneking-pubs.co.uk/pubs/wiltshire/red-lion

The Red Lion is the only inn in the world located inside a prehistoric stone circle. The Avebury monument which actually comprises of three stone circles dates from between 4000 and 2400BC. This legend-shrouded location has an undoubted aura of magic and mystery and several ghosts are said to reside both within and without the ancient property.

The whitewashed walls and dark, thatched roof of the pub present a strange contrast to the colossal stones that encircle

The Red Lion is the only inn in the world located inside a prehistoric stone circle.

it. The original building dates from the early 1600s, and was a farmhouse until 1802, when it was licensed and started trading as a coaching inn.

There have been reports of at least five ghosts at *The Red Lion* but the most enduring story is that of Florrie whose presence is enshrined in local folklore, and popularised by television programmes such as *Most Haunted*. In the seventeenth century, during the English Civil War, Florrie's husband is said to have returned unannounced from the conflict and caught his wife in the arms of another man. He shot his rival dead, slit his wife's throat and disposed of her body down the well.

The most enduring story is that of Florrie who was murdered by her husband and disposed of down this well.

Many years later when the well was excavated female skeletal remains were found lying 86 feet down at the bottom of the shaft. Florrie's ghost has been seen emerging from and disappearing into the old well, which is now glassed over to serve both as a curiosity and a drinks table. Bearded customers in particular appear to attract Florrie's attention. On one occasion a chandelier in the restaurant suddenly began to spin round at an alarming speed. When the manager was summoned, he nodded knowingly seeing the man sitting directly underneath sported a bushy beard.

Another story relates to a man stabbed to death in the cellar. Staff have reported feeling his angry presence to this day. One paranormal investigator unaware of the pub's history experienced a vision of a bald man who appeared to be bleeding and acting violently; thrusting forward a number of times with a knife. A container of bottle tops was also flung violently down the open hatch of the cellar.

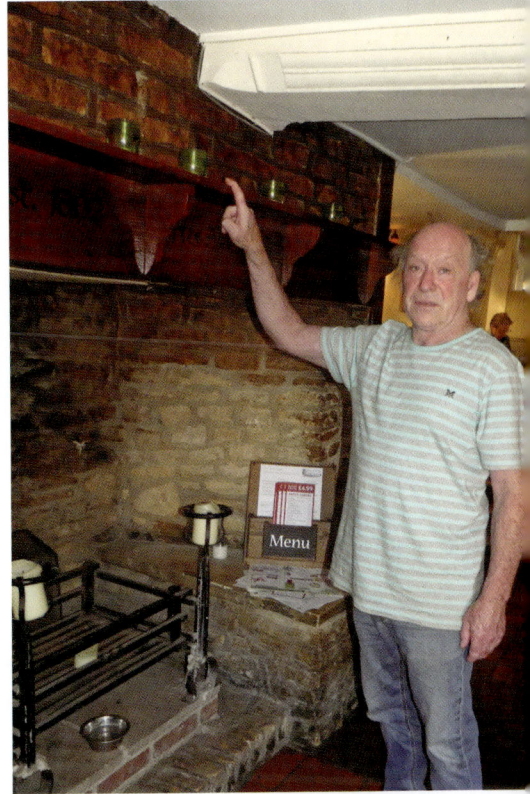

Regular customer Dermot indicating the glass candleholder he saw fly off the shelf and across the bar.

Other parts of the 400-year-old building are also haunted. The Avenue Room upstairs is now used as staff quarters. Previously, when it was one of the letting rooms, guests reported seeing the ghosts of two children cowering in a corner crying. They were often in the company of an equally ethereal woman writing at the table either oblivious to or unconcerned by the children's evident distress.

Dermot also witnessed one of these teaspoons jump from its saucer before hitting the ceiling and skimming across the room.

Paul, another regular, has several times witnessed children and dogs becoming distressed immediately on entering the front door.

Karyn Pithouse, (seen here pulling a pint for a customer) has a wealth of ghost stories and has featured some of them in an information leaflet.

When no one was present in the bar a container of bottle tops was flung violently down the open hatch of the cellar at a paranormal investigating team.

Dermot, one of the regular customers, tells the story of how he saw a glass candleholder fall from a mantel shelf to the floor and on another occasion saw it fly off the shelf and across the bar. He also witnessed a teaspoon jump from a saucer before hitting the ceiling and skimming across the room. Paul, another regular, confirmed Dermot's stories saying he often saw children physically frightened on approaching the building and becoming distressed when their parents tried to encourage them to enter. He has several times witnessed dogs who whimper when just inside the entrance, obviously scared to venture further.

Karyn Pithouse, who has worked at The Red Lion for a number of years, also has a wealth of ghost stories and has incorporated some of them into an information leaflet. This includes the story of a phantom carriage, drawn by ghostly horses heard by staff and customers alike clattering across the inn's courtyard.

Another enduring story is of a phantom carriage, drawn by ghostly horses heard by staff and customers alike clattering across the inn's courtyard.

Atop a steep valley
in this picturesque
hamlet, stands the
fifteenth-century
Cross Guns pub
whose terraced
gardens offer a
splendid view of
the Avoncliff
triple-arched canal
aqueduct.

Avoncliff
Cross Guns
Bradford-on-Avon BA15 2HB

Tel: 01225 862335

www.crossgunsavoncliff.com

Atop a steep valley in this picturesque hamlet, stands the fifteenth-century Cross Guns pub. The terraced gardens offer a splendid view of the Avoncliff triple arched aqueduct, designed and built by John Rennie and John Thomas between 1797 and 1801. This impressive stone edifice which carries the Kennet & Avon canal over the River Avon and Box railway ranks as one of the most magnificent of Britain's artificial waterways constructions.

For more than thirty years staff and customers at this special pub have reported sightings of three very different ghosts; a monk-like figure, a bargee and an apparition in the form of an elderly Victorian lady wearing a blue-grey dress.

Staff laying tables in the lounge, in preparation for evening diners, have spoken of seeing a monk like figure standing by the inglenook fireplace. On occasion he is seen disappearing into, or standing close to a former entrance to the cellars which is now blocked up. The cellars were said to link to a tunnel leading down to the canal and many people have claimed to feel 'uncomfortably nervous' near this mysterious entrance.

Less often encountered is an elderly gentleman, thought to be an eighteenth-century bargee. When staff member Christine first saw him she thought he was a customer who had been chatting to Ken Roberts the landlord at the time. Mentioning it moments later to another member of staff her colleague looked surprised and told her she must be mistaken, as she had just left that area and Ken was quite alone.

Of all the phantoms reputed to haunt the Cross Guns, the Blue Lady is most frequently seen. When encountered, she is always described as dressed in blue or grey-blue in the style of the Victorian period. She has been sighted in various rooms

Originally built in Tudor times as a private residence, it became an inn in the 1600s known as The Carpenter's Arms providing respite for travellers and drovers using the ford across the river.

Above: Staff laying tables in the lounge, in preparation for evening diners, have spoken of seeing a monk-like figure standing here by the inglenook fireplace.

Right: On occasion the phantom cleric is seen disappearing into, or standing close to this former mysterious entry.

Anglers fishing on the banks of the Avon and boaters who have moored on the canal attest to fleeting glimpses of the blue lady as they make their ascent from the valley floor up the steps to the pub. She is said to stand quite motionless looking down at the river from the garden.

in the pub and in the gardens. Anglers fishing on the banks of the Avon and boaters who have moored on the canal attest to fleeting glimpses of her as they make their ascent from the valley floor up the steps to the pub. She is said to stand quite motionless looking down at the river from the garden. You can imagine the look of shock, when visitors reach the pub only to be told by staff that the Victorian lady dressed in blue you have just described, is probably one of our ghosts.

At a time when there were no roads to speak of in Avoncliff, folk used a footpath leading down from the top of the valley, behind the pub and on to the river below. The route of that old trail passed directly through what is now the toilets and where the Blue Lady is most often encountered. Originally she was seen gliding through the wall of the ladies toilet but current landlady Samantha Birks said recent alterations to the structure of the pub means she now manifests passing through the gents!

One of the oldest buildings in Avoncliff, the twin-gabled central section of The Cross Guns is believed to date from the 1490s.

One of the oldest buildings in Avoncliff, the twin-gabled central section of the Cross Guns is believed to date from the 1490s, and the style of the central inglenook fireplace seems to confirm this. It was originally a private residence but with the construction of the East wing in the early 1600s, it became an inn known as The Carpenter's Arms providing respite for travellers and drovers using the ford across the river. It was later also used by quarrymen and millworkers.

The rural serenity of Avoncliff was disturbed from 1794, when the 9th (Bradford-on-Avon) Battalion of the Wiltshire Rifle Volunteers was formed and a rifle range established alongside the canal. It was shortly after this The Carpenter's Arms was renamed the Cross Guns, both in recognition of the formation of the local yeomanry and as a salutary warning to rioting agricultural labourers of the time that retribution was close by!

Current landlady Samantha Birks, seen here serving customers on the decking high above the river valley has lived amicably with the blue lady for a couple of years.

Beckhampton
The Waggon & Horses

Beckhampton, Marlborough SN8 1QJ

Tel: 01672 539418

www.waggonandhorsesbeckhampton.co.uk

This most attractive thatched pub was built in 1669 primarily as a coaching inn and is the subject of many ghost stories.

This most attractive thatched pub was built in 1669 primarily as a coaching inn and initially bore the name The Black Bear. In 1724 this was changed to The Hare & Hounds, possibly in response to hare coursing which was prevalent in the area. Finally in 1823, it became The Waggon & Horses, reflecting the custom it received from wagoners and drovers who frequented the inn when driving their livestock to markets in London. In addition to accommodation the inn offered grazing land for cattle plus stabling and a smithy.

Donna, the current assistant manager organises paranormal evenings at the pub with help from the team at 'Bump in the Night' but she says you need to be quick to join in because as

The most enduring tale is of an evocative manifestation seen outside the pub on winter nights when a ghostly coach and horses rattles over the stones and stops before the front door.

soon as they are announced on Facebook available places are snapped up. Donna herself has experienced strange things happening at the pub. Fairy lights are mysteriously turned on and off and when locking up of an evening, when nobody else is around, she often sees unexplained movements from the corner of her eye and once heard somebody call out YOU! in a very loud voice, but nobody was there. She is hoping that the newly installed CCTV system will reveal the origin of a shadow she has seen walking into the office.

The phantom of an elderly woman dressed in a white blouse or smock appears in the bar and is thought to be a previous proprietor.

As things are at the moment Donna is reluctant to enter the kitchen because of bad vibes and will not look back at the building after she has left the pub. Some of the other girls share Donna's unease and have confirmed similar strange happenings. During the paranormal evenings two particular spirits have made themselves known. One is a female called Ida and the other a little boy named Thomas.

Historical reports of paranormal manifestations include two tales of other ghosts who appear from time to time in the main bar. One is an elderly woman dressed in a white blouse or smock who is thought to have been a previous proprietor. The second spirit is a tall man dressed in a Victorian-style suit smoking a pipe and leaning against the fireplace. Some witnesses have seen a little dog crouched at his feet and were aware of a strong odour of tobacco smoke lingering for some time after the ghost disappeared.

The ghost of a tall man dressed in a Victorian style suit is seen smoking a pipe and leaning against the fireplace, a strong odour of tobacco smoke lingering after he has disappeared.

During the paranormal evenings two spirits have made themselves known, a female called Ida and a little boy named Thomas.

The old highway that passes the pub was once part of The Great West Road linking London and Bristol. The journey on horseback or by stagecoach would take two days, crossing the coldest stretch of the Marlborough Downs at Beckhampton around the halfway point. On severe winter nights The Waggon & Horses was a most welcome sight and potential stopover for many a weary traveller including seasoned ones like Charles Dickens who featured the pub in *The Bag Man's Story* from *Pickwick Papers*.

The most enduring tale of all is of an evocative manifestation seen outside the pub on winter nights when a ghostly coach and horses rattles over the stones and stops before the front door. The suggestion is the coach party succumbed to hypothermia one night, trapped in blizzards and snowdrifts on the Downs.

Bradford-on-Avon
The Canal Tavern

49 Frome Road, Bradford-on-Avon BA15 1LE

Tel: 01225 866100

www.canaltavern.co.uk

The Canal Tavern at Bradford-on-Avon is a fascinating architectural jigsaw puzzle backing on to the Kennet & Avon Canal immediately below Bradford lock. This atmospheric old pub has developed from a collection of buildings constructed over time from locally quarried freestone. The complex has provided various commercial uses as boatyard, warehouse, stables for towpath horses, dwelling and hostelry. At the time of writing this pub is undergoing a 'refresh' and may well look different when you visit.

The Canal Tavern was sold to Wadworth Brewery in 1885 for £402 with fixtures priced at £63.

The earliest licensee of the tavern was Robert Edmonds in 1851 who is listed as occupier, boat builder and beer retailer. The wharf at Bradford-on-Avon was the busiest on the Kennet & Avon Canal during the 1850s but, in addition to his other

The pub today is a fascinating architectural jigsaw puzzle developed from a collection of buildings constructed over time from locally quarried freestone.

Although only officially operating as a pub since 1851 the old beams and wall thicknesses confirm it to be a much older building.
Below: The old fireplace is decorated with the traditional canal ware floral art.

duties, Robert found time for a sideline, escorting 'ladies of the town' by barge along the canal to The Carpenter's Arms (now the Cross Guns) in order to warm the spirits of Avoncliff boatmen, quarry workers and soldiers, whose camp had been established at Avoncliff for more than fifty years.

During the First World War the narrow boat *Bittern* was purchased by The Red Cross, for use as hospital transport to convey wounded soldiers to Avoncliff. The barge was moored at Bradford Wharf and the tow horse that pulled it was stabled at The Canal Tavern.

Such a busy place naturally has its share of recorded paranormal incidents. Many claims have been made of seeing the spectre of an elderly gentleman, thought to be a departed former landlord quietly puffing away on a clay pipe in what is now the kitchen of the pub. There is also a very strange cold spot at the bottom of the stairs which has been identified as an area of poltergeist activity.

Canal tow horses like this were stabled at the tavern.

Modern day narrow boat enthusiasts at Bradf Wharf waiting their turn to enter the lock.

In 2009 a previous landlord and landlady were standing outside the pub when they saw a shadow inside crossing in front of the living room window. Shadows were also reportedly seen in the utility room and incongruous church music heard in the area of the bar. Today the pub caters mainly for walkers, boaters and visitors to the wonderfully historic town.

Castle Eaton
Red Lion
The Street, Castle Eaton SN6 6JZ

Tel: 01285 810280

www.red-lion.co.uk

Proud to be the first pub on the Thames, the large gardens of
the Red Lion extend down to the river making it ideally positioned for canoeists or walkers on the Thames Path. The river-
bank scene is also visible from the 32-seat conservatory.

Although the setting is tranquil, Melody Lyall who took over
as landlady in 2002, has experienced a wealth of ghostly
encounters. Things seem to have settled down somewhat
now although some guests say they have been aware of a
presence in their room sitting on the bed.

Things are mostly tranquil
now in this traditional
village pub.

Most of the earlier reported happenings followed a familiar course; things were moved and broken, sudden unexplained changes in temperature felt and the sound of heavy footsteps heard on the wooden floors leading through areas that are no longer accessible.

Most alarming of all was the night Melody was asleep in bed and felt a man's hand grab her shoulder and shake her quite violently. She awoke

Melody Lyall, who took over as landlady in 2002, has experienced a wealth of ghostly encounters.

Below: The modern clock above the entrance to the bar is a replacement for the antique one staff witnessed flying off the wall one Halloween night.

to see the ghost of a man dressed in a coat with a distinctive white edged collar and remembered he was wearing buckled shoes – but he didn't have a face! Another time Melody saw the ghost he appeared to be hanging on the wall but she concluded he might have been standing on the floor level as it was during an earlier period of the pub's history.

Melody's son has also witnessed mysterious events. He saw a glass move on its own in his bedroom before it hit him on the head and smashed all over his bed. He also reported seeing the ghostly figure of a little girl plus that of a dog and even managed to photograph the faceless man but the print turned out to be too grainy to see any detail.

Most of the earlier reported happenings followed a familiar course when things were moved and broken and sudden unexplained changes in temperature felt.

Former owners of the pub reported seeing the faceless man on the top floor and in one of the double B&B bedrooms. On a recent Halloween night staff witnessed a clock flying off the wall in the bar and when they entered the kitchen the following morning all the health and safety signs had been ripped off the wall and scattered about the floor.

The large gardens of this lovely old pub extend down to the fledgling River Thames.

Chippenham
Bear Hotel

12 Market Place, Chippenham SN15 3HJ

Tel: 01249 650647

The magnificent town house that became the Bear Hotel was built by Chippenham builder John Provis in 1750 on what was believed to be the site of a medieval convent. Dominating the old market place in the heart of this historic town the building was still a private residence in 1812. By 1850 it had been remodelled as an inn named the Bear from the heraldic sign of Richard Neville, Earl of Warwick (1428-71).

With the exception of one spooky bar stool that regulars refuse to use, paranormal activities seem to be confined to the cellar and one or more of the upstairs rooms. Most notable of these happenings being the cellar door which is reported to open itself to reveal a figure in the doorway and footsteps often accompany this spectral vision.

Dominating the old market place in the heart of historic Chippenham the Bear Hotel was still a private residence in 1812 but remodelled as an inn in 1850.

Joe (Giuseppe) Kennedy, the current landlord whose cousin Darren had something thrown at him whilst working in the cellar.

Joe (Giuseppe) Kennedy the current landlord said his cousin Darren, whilst working in the cellar, had something thrown at him. He also said when TV paranormal investigators were filming in the hotel a lady called out 'Giuseppe', a name only his grandmother had ever called him. At one point something spooked the investigators so much they all ran out of the building.

A bricked up archway in the cellar is thought to be the entrance to an old tunnel whose subterranean passage leads to St Andrew's church. Others have suggested the tunnel might even lead all the way to link up with the cellars of Lacock Abbey 3 miles to the south.

As far as the upstairs is concerned a barman heard loud voices one night coming from an empty room. He checked

The door to these cellar steps is reported to fleetingly open by itself revealing a figure in the doorway.

This bricked-up archway in the cellar is thought to be the entrance to an old tunnel whose subterranean passage leads to St Andrew's church.

The huge front doors of the Bear Hotel open directly onto the historic market place.

The old cobbled coaching yard once echoed with the sound of horse hooves and clattering carriages.

but not a living soul was present. Coincidentally, one of the housekeeping staff walking to work one morning distinctly saw a woman in grey close the curtains of that room. She later learned the room had not been occupied that day or the night before. It has been suggested she might have seen the ghost of one of the nuns from the former convent.

Corsham
The Flemish Weaver

63 High St, Corsham SN13 0EZ

Tel: 01249 701929

The building, which dates to 1625, became a pub in 1645.

In 2010, shortly after taking over this seventeenth-century pub landlady Dawn McHugh called in the ghostbusters. She had been attacked by an angry spirit who tripped her up, sending her flying down the stairs. The drama happened on Easter Monday, only days after Dawn moved into the pub with her husband Mac. It meant she ended up in hospital for the day until doctors were satisfied that her suspected fractured skull was, in fact, bad bruising. Mrs McHugh said:

'The first time it happened I thought nothing of it but it happened a second time, just a week later, when I was putting up some curtains I felt something strong pulling me around.'

She blamed the ghost for this and another incident when her ironing board crashed to the ground.

The happenings at the pub, which dates from 1625, so shocked the couple they enlisted the help of Corsham spiritualist Kim Healy, who organised an in house séance of seven people. Drama occurred again, however, when a butter plate was flung from the table where they were sitting, smashing on the floor. Sensing the presence of an angry spirit Dawn said:

The Flemish Weaver is an intriguing pub and full of character that reveals itself slowly through its many nooks and crannies.

'Three of us had picked up that it was a man who carried a stick and he was chasing children. Another picked up a woman who

we think was his wife. Something was holding him here and he didn't want to go.'

Staff at the pub also say they witnessed strange sights. Waitress Loretta Butterworth, nineteen, said:

'Once, I was sitting having lunch when I saw the outline of a man. Another time I saw the man standing by the window.'

Alex, the current assistant manager, has observed many unexplained happenings including the sound of a lady crying in the toilets when there is nobody there, glasses moving, bottles falling to the floor and the front door opening and closing on its own. He also said one customer went white when he heard a voice in his ear saying get out! get out!

Alex, the current assistant manager, has observed many unexplained happenings, glasses moving and bottles falling to the floor.

This seventeenth-century ale house gets its name from the Flemish weavers who fled from religious persecution in Flan-

The front door of this ancient pub is known to open and close on its own with the sound of a clicking latch.

ders and took up residence in the row of cottages adjoining the pub which greatly enhanced Corsham's woollen industry.

The Flemish Weaver is an intriguing pub and full of character that reveals itself slowly through its many nooks and crannies. The garden in particular, where the original pack horses were stabled, is a pleasant and unexpected surprise. There's a focus on quality service and real ale, where all four pumps regularly change.

The original packhorse yard has been transformed into a garden presenting a pleasant and unexpected surprise.

Corsham
The Royal Oak

72 High Street, Corsham SN13 0HF

Tel: 01249 713607

www.corshamroyaloak.co.uk

The first record of this town centre pub was in 1867 when Thomas White, a cooper, held the licence. A notable feature of the inn is the elegant staircase leading up to the function room and guest rooms. The apparition of a stylishly young woman is seen ascending the spiral staircase flicking her long skirt coquettishly as she does. This is thought to be the ghost of a girl who had fallen from the landing sometime in the 1970s. It is said she fell backwards from the balcony and broke her neck on the stairs. Looking at the situation it is not clear how someone could fall accidenty which suggests foul play might have been involved.

The Royal Oak in the centre of the high street has been the scene of numerous paranormal sightings.

The elegant staircase is reputedly the scene of a fatality which might not have been an accident.

Former landlord Nick Taylor claimed to have seen several ghosts in his pub but always in his peripheral vision. He said he saw the woman at the top of the stairs flicking her floor length skirt so often that after a while it didn't even make him flinch. Gareth Hughes, a member of the *Twelfth Hour Investigations* team from Bradford on Avon said he detected a depressed spirit in room three, which is one of the guest B&B rooms. The visiting team also recorded abnormal temperature changes in the flat above the pub.

Unconcerned regular customers I spoke to were more interested in beer and football than spooky spirits.

Jo Perry, who has worked at the pub for a number of years said one regular B&B guest has complained about having the duvet pulled off the bed in the middle of the night. Jo also says she is regularly aware of a male figure dressed in black in the kitchen area. She only glimpses him out of the corner of her eye and sometimes tells him sternly to go away! To which he complies.

Jo Perry.

There are stories of three very different ghosts making their presence felt in this traditional and extensive country pub.

Corsley Heath
The Royal Oak

Corsley Heath BA12 7PR

Tel: 01373 832238

www.theroyaloakcorsley.co.uk

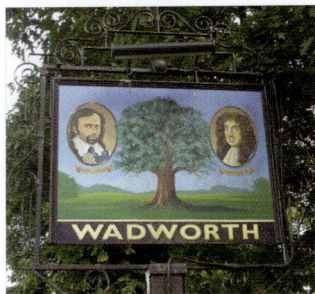

There are stories of three very different ghosts making their presence felt in this traditional and extensive country pub standing alongside the main road at the edge of Corsley village. Two are seen only as amorphous shapes; a black one in one of the bedrooms and a white one in the kitchen.

The tale relating to the oldest phantom has its origins in the middle ages when the building was run as a hospice. It was owned and administered by holy men of Long Leat Friary, on whose land the stately home of Longleat was later built. The

On duty one night Acacia (seen here) heard her daughter Lily running up and down the stairs to her flat above. When she checked she discovered Lily was sound asleep in bed.

A dog named Willow belonging to licencees Kerry and Mark heads straight for this spot when he enters the dining room and barks at the wall where the warming pan is displayed.

friars at the hospice offered food and lodgings to passing pilgrims and other travellers. One of the friars however proved to be neither honest nor holy. After plying visitors with ale until they were insensible he searched their belongings and pockets for money or valuables. This crooked cleric also stole church funds provided by the Friary for administration of the hospice.

This miscreant monk was eventually caught and subjected to the most unholy of punishments, being walled up alive in the cellar and left to die. His bones are still there and his ghost is seen from time to time. There is a particular spot on the wall where his face appears then fades away. The bar staff are adamant it is not just shadows playing on the rough stone surface. The area has been painted over but the face continues to appear.

A more regular sighting is that of a lady dressed in a dark full length dress and wearing a wide brimmed hat. Seen striding confidently about the pub she has an aura of elegance and culture and exudes an air of authority. A former landlady reported a barman was ascending the stairs one day when the ghost appeared on the landing heading down. He stepped aside to let her pass as naturally as he would with a real person. When she reached the foot of the stairs he watched as she walked through the door. Thinking back on the situation later he said he was aware it was a ghost but the incident seemed so natural it didn't frighten him. Staff over a period of at least twenty-five years have reported seeing the lady. There is speculation she might be a former landlady or perhaps a guest who stayed at the inn towards the end of the stagecoach era but nobody really knows.

The stables, now incorporated into the pub, are a reminder of the days when The Royal Oak was a coaching inn and well-known hangout for highway men.

The third ghost is the most enigmatic appearing in the kitchen as a white flimsy apparition or 'thing'. Insubstantial it might be but this spirit gets the blame for turning the lights on and off with annoying regularity. One of the kitchen staff said during broad daylight the lights still come on of their own accord.

Devizes
The Bear Hotel
The Market Place, Devizes SN10 1HS

Tel: 01380 722444

When I spoke to the manageress of this renowned hotel she said it had its share of ghost related incidents in the past but all was tranquil now. Indeed, having left a previous haunted establishment, the peaceful ambience of this splendid old inn was a deciding factor in attracting her to take it on.

Built in 1599, The Bear stands boldly at the top of the town above the Buttercross on the opposite side of the old market place from The Black Swan.

The Bear Inn in Devizes was not only one of the grandest and most celebrated inns in Wiltshire; it was one of the grandest and most celebrated in the country. Built in 1599, it stands boldly at the top of the town above the Buttercross, on the opposite side of the old market place from the Black Swan. It was originally called The Bear & Ragged Staff, a reference to the crest of the Earls of Warwick and later The Black Bear, presumably to clearly differentiate it from The White Bear in Monday Market Street. By the mid seventeenth century it had a bowling alley and was set in ornamental grounds. Throughout the hotel today there is an abundance of wood panelling, wooden floors, heavy oak beams and open fires.

In 1857 the ornate frontage was relocated to the back of the building and can be seen today from the inn's courtyard garden.

One of the barmen I spoke too said a customer inexplicably disappeared whilst he was serving him.

Following the Battle of Sedgemoor in 1685, both senior judges, Jeffreys and Col Kirke lodged here. There is still a Judge's Cupboard in the ancient arched cellars, where their special wines were kept. Earlier paranormal reference described an unexplained strong male presence in the cellars. George Long in his book *English Inns and Roadhouses* (1937) refers to a scratched sentence on a window in the inn which reads: '*John Blome, Mircht,* (Merchant?) *on his way from London to Bath for execution, February 23rd, 1766*'. It is said the condemned man and his escort arrived rather late and the keyholder of the town lock-up refused to admit them, so they put up at The Bear, where the doomed man left this pathetic record behind. He was duly hanged the next day which led me to wonder if it might be the spirit of this miscreant merchant who returns to the place where he spent his last night on earth?

The old coaching route from London which ran nearby was subject to the attentions of highwaymen and other outlaws. When the road was re-routed through Devizes, The Bear became a hub of activity. At the height of the stagecoach era, when the inn was owned by William Halcomb, new assembly rooms were added and up to 30 coaches a day stopped here.

Visiting psychic investigators *Spiriteam* said room 4 was the most haunted but today everything is peace and tranquility.

Many eighteenth-century notables stayed at The Bear including David Garrick, Dr Johnson, Sir Joshua Reynolds, Richard Brinsley Sheridan and Sarah Siddons, for whom one of the rooms is named. Royalty also numbered among the illustrious visitors and for many years, it was maintained that Queen Charlotte, who lodged here in 1817, returned to haunt the place.

Those who witnessed the apparition described her as wearing an off the shoulder dress with long lace cuffs and a wide skirt. The description fits a number of the queen's portraits and one source says: '*it could almost be certain it is she*'. However, there is no explanation as to why the queen should haunt the inn. She died on 17 November 1818, the year after her visit to Devizes, but she breathed her last in the presence of her eldest

Sarah Siddons, the leading actress of her day.

son, the Prince Regent, who was holding her hand as she sat in an armchair at the family's country retreat, Dutch House in Surrey, now known as Kew Palace. There are other reports of a more modestly dressed 'grey lady' seen wandering the corridors who is thought to be a coach passenger who died before completing her journey.

The atmospheric cellar bar where tunnels are previously thought to have led to the castle.

This most fashionable of hostelries attracted a succession of notable landlords including Thomas Lawrence who came here in 1772. His young son, also named Thomas, delighted guests by sketching their portraits and reciting poetry. Thomas Lawrence junior became the greatest portrait painter of his time. In 1815 he was knighted and in 1820 became President of the Royal Academy. Despite attracting visitors from the higher echelons of society to The Bear, Lawrence senior was declared bankrupt in 1780, claiming he had lost over £1000 since taking the inn because of having soldiers billeted on him: *'up to 70 at a time' for weeks and months'*.

The stagecoach business effectively ended with the arrival of the Great Western Railway. To add to the problem, Devizes was bypassed and a branch line to the town was not built until 1857. Despite the lack of a main line station the town continued to prosper as a principal agricultural centre and the same year its importance was recognized by the introduction of a corn exchange built next to The Bear. The construction involved removing some of the inn's ancillary buildings no longer required now coaches had ceased to stop here. Among the casualties were the assembly rooms and the ornate frontage which was relocated to the back of the building and can be seen today from the inn's courtyard garden.

A more recent ghost story comes from 1965 when a barman heard loud voices coming from a room he was sure was empty. After investigating, he found he had been correct and the room was indeed unoccupied. On another occasion, one of the housekeeping staff was outside the inn when she saw a grey figure closing the curtains in a room she knew was vacant. Entering the hotel she went straight to the room to double-check but found it to be empty. A further account concerns a lady who had a 'timeslip' experience while standing outside the hotel. She witnessed a dinner scene on an upper floor where maids wearing mobcaps passed to and fro as if serving at table and waiters carried decanters on trays. She checked with staff but there had been no such party that day.

A few years ago the hotel was visited by paranormal investigators *Spiriteam*, accompanied by Rachel and Sarah from *Night Frights Paranormal*. Sarah, who is sensitive, reported evidence of a number of ghosts; in particular she began picking up on a young, dirty looking urchin boy who she felt was named Tom. The team found bedroom 4 to be the most active when a motion sensor they positioned near the doorway was set off twice when no one was near. A bed appeared to be vibrating and a strange black streak was seen by two people, also near the doorway.

The old town lock-up where miscreant merchant John Blome arrived too late to spend his last night on earth and had to stay at The Bear instead, presumably locked in the vaulted cellar.

In the cellars some of the team had a feeling of immense sadness reducing one of them to tears and others reported feeling a big drop in temperature even though they were otherwise comfortably warm throughout the night. Their last investigation area was 'The Siddons Room' where they were told there had been a death at some time. The ghost hunter's equipment including a string of bells, a balloon and an LED ball were used as trigger objects. The ball, which has to be moved to set off the lights, set off twice and there was some activity detected on the other devices. In addition there was some very unusual activity on other specialist apparatus including Rem Pods, Mel and EMF meters.

At the end of my visit I spoke with one of the barmen who has worked here for ten years. He said during his early time tending bar he reached behind him to get a tonic water for a customer but when he turned back the man had disappeared.

he hotel fronts the town square overlooking the
pot where the town gallows once stood.

Devizes
Black Swan Inn
25-26 Market Place, Devizes SN10 1JQ

Tel: 01380 727777

www.blackswandevizes.co.uk

At six am on a November morning in 2017 the mobile phones
of all the staff and guests at the Black Swan went off simultaneously and a man sleeping in room 4 was thrown from his
bed by an invisible force. This was the latest in a series of
continually reported paranormal activities. In 2009 Pam Lugg,
landlady at the time, summarised her experience in an inter-
view with ghost hunter David Scanlan:

*'We hear chairs moving on their own in the function room, foot-
steps in empty corridors, the click of latches as heavy doors open
and close on their own. People have also seen a shadowy figure*

At six am on a November morning in 2017 the mobile phones of all the staff and guests at the hotel went off simultaneously.

that moves past the reception area and heads down the stairs to the cellar.'

This last spectre is thought to be notorious horse trader and suspected highwayman Ambrose Saintsbury. The Black Swan was built as a traditional coaching inn in 1732 on the site of an earlier hostelry called The Nags Head which was owned by Saintsbury who appears to have led a double life as a respectable inn keeper and ruthless highwayman. Saintsbury was reputed to keep his horses stabled in the cellar tunnels along with a change of clothing. His ghostly apparition is often accompanied by a woman whose identity is unknown and he has even report-

Room 4 at the Black Swan has a reputation as being one of the most haunted bedrooms in the country.

edly been seen sitting astride a horse in the cellars.

The labyrinthine cellar complex dates from the 1600s and comprises of five chambers leading off a central passage. The rear of the cellar has been bricked up, blocking access to what is believed some extra 100 feet or so of underground tunnel running beneath the inn yard. In 1999, John Girven local historian, removed some bricks whilst investigating the suspected tunnel and this act marked the start of the severe haunting of the cellar area including reports of hot and cold spots, people being touched, shadowy figures and outlines, light anomalies, and unexplained tapping noises.

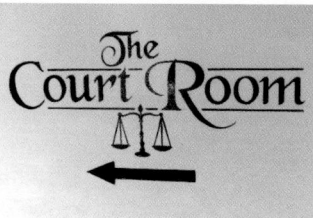

The Court Room

In the former court room some felons were sentenced to hang for crimes considered minor today.

Upstairs, in room 4, guests and staff members have witnessed the ghost of a young woman wearing a long flowing dress who is said to appear through one of the walls. After sitting for a second or two staring out of the window she disappears

The present-day function room where poltergeist activity is reported including chairs moving on their own.

A number of people have seen a shadowy figure moving past the reception area heading down the stairs to the cellar.

through the opposite wall. Some say she may be the phantom of a woman who became trapped and perished during a fire in the hotel in the mid-1700s. Understandably these sightings have unnerved some guests who have requested a move to a different room. However, it has not discouraged others and the hotel has numerous booking requests from prospective guests specifically asking for room 4.

The present-day function room was a regular meeting place for local freemasons and trade guilds. The explanation of poltergeist activity here may originate from the time it served regularly as a court room where some felons were sentenced to hang for crimes considered minor today. The hotel fronts the town square overlooking the spot where the town gallows once stood.

Parts of the labyrinthine cellar area are subject to various phenomena including light anomalies, hot and cold spots, people being touched, shadowy figures and outlines and unexplained tapping noises.

The imposing red brick Castle Hotel with its attractive mansard roof was opened in 1768. Phantom music has been heard coming from the former assembly room located above the coaching entrance.

Devizes
The Castle Hotel

New Park Street, Devizes SN10 1DS

Tel: 01380 727981

The imposing red brick Castle Hotel was opened by John Oak in 1768. Its architectural attractiveness is enhanced by the double sloping mansard roof. The lower slope, steeper than the upper, is punctured by dormer windows creating an additional floor of habitable space. There is also a classic Bath stone portico surmounted by a profusion of flowers in the summer.

On the left of the building is the former coaching entrance leading through to the stable yard. Above this was the assembly room where, in Georgian times, balls and parties were held. Over the intervening years, phantom music has been heard in this area. The internal space has subsequently been converted into three letting rooms, numbers 7, 8 and 9.

The classic Bath stone portico is surmounted by a profusion of flowers in the summer.

The assistant manager who has worked here for 10 years has often heard heavy footsteps above the bar and dining room when there are no resident guests.

The young son of a former manager used to stand completely transfixed staring into this mirror.

One family were staying here a couple of years ago when the mother saw a girl she thought was her daughter go into the bathroom. However, when checking, she found the child asleep in bed. Despite having booked for a week the family left the following day.

Cameron Newman, the assistant manager who has worked here for ten years related this story and tales of other numerous unexplained happenings. Once, walking along the corridor outside room 12, he heard the voice of a young girl call out his name. On another occasion, in the same place, staff member Helen had a similar experience. When downstairs in the bar, Cameron has often heard footsteps walking along corridors on the first floor during periods when the rooms are empty.

The inn backs directly on to St Mary's churchyard. The present church building was started by Bishop Roger of Salisbury in 1143. Sometimes, where the surface level of ancient churchyards are raised – as this one – it can indicate the location of a mass grave dating from the plague years. This might be the case here because Devizes suffered great mortality from the plague in 1607. A former general manager of The Castle Hotel was walking his dog in the graveyard one night and could see the televisions were on in rooms 15 and 16 of the inn; although both rooms were unoccupied at that time. The same man had an unnerving experience with his two-year-old daughter. If he was with her near room 14, she would scream and refuse to enter.

The two year old daughter of another manager used to scream whenever she was taken near the entrance to this room.

Another manager in charge during Cameron's time had a problem with his two children. During the night they would wake upset because they said they could see an old lady sitting on their bed but when the parents investigated there was no one there. On one of the landings there is a huge mirror which seemed to mesmerise the little boy who used to stand completely transfixed staring into it.

On other occasions staff have reported objects vanishing only to reappear later in different locations around the hotel. Ghostly goings-on recorded in 2011 included a glass flying from a shelf and landing in pieces on the ground.

Whilst walking his dog in the graveyard one night a former general manager of The Castle Inn could see the televisions were on in rooms 15 & 16 of the inn, although both rooms were unoccupied at that time.

Located in the central town area of Devizes, The Three Crowns Inn is currently a flagship pub for Wadworth brewery.

The Three Crowns

Maryport Street, Devizes SN10 1AG

Tel: 01380 722331

www.threecrownsdevizes.co.uk

Located in the central town area of Devizes, The Three Crowns Inn is currently a flagship pub for Wadworth brewery. Recently extensively modernised it still retains the original beams of the historical seventeenth-century building.

There are two ghost stories involving women said to haunt the pub; one is very sad, the other more wistful. The first involves a bride, name unknown, said to have committed suicide in the building after being jilted at the altar and her pallid form appears from time to time. The second is the spirit of Mrs Phipp, proud landlady of the pub in the early twentieth-century.

In the bar is an early photograph of Mrs Phipp standing outside the pub having lavishly decorated it with flowers to celebrate the coronation of King George V and his consort, Queen Mary. A clipping from the local paper is mounted with the photograph and reads: *'Decorations at the Three Crowns Brewery Devizes On Coronation Day June 22nd 1911'*.

'This was regarded as being one of the prettiest and most effective decorations in the West of England. Mrs Phipp, who

When paranormal investigators visited the pub it was in the former tea rooms area they found most activity.

carried out the scheme, had been working since the beginning of the year making the flowers etc. and there were nearly 6,000 separate blooms used. The four windows represented Spring, Summer, Autumn and Winter. The decorative scheme was greatly admired, not only by townspeople but by visitors.'

It seems Mrs Phipp so loved the pub she is reluctant to leave. Sheila, one of the housekeepers has reported doors slamming and feeling someone poking her in the back. Cassey, one of the bar staff, was relaxing with other members of the team one evening after closing time when she heard the sounds of chains rattling at the back door.

One evening after closing time Cassey reported hearing the sounds of chains rattling at the back door.

For many years the pub has been divided into two halves with the right hand side housing the early brewery. This facil-

The pallid form of a bride who committed suicide in the building after being jilted at the altar appears from time to time.

Recently extensively modernised The Three Crowns still retains the original beams and some of the exposed brickwork of the historical seventeenth-century building.

ity was closed in 1919 when the business was taken over by Wadworth and the right half eventually became Emily's Tea Room. When paranormal investigators visited The Three Crowns it was in the former tea room area they found most activity. Following a recent extensive modernisation this part of the building has been turned into letting rooms and staff accommodation for visiting Wadworth managers.

Mrs Phipp standing outside the pub having lavishly decorated it with flowers to celebrate the coronation of King George V and his consort, Queen Mary.

Devizes

White Bear

Monday Market Street, Devizes SN10 1DN

Tel: 01380 727588

www.whitebeardevizes.co.uk

Reputed to be the oldest pub in Devizes, the White Bear was trading as an inn called The Talbot, fifty years before Henry VIII was born.

Travelling east along New Park Street (A361), immediately beyond The Castle Inn, the road takes a sweeping 90 degree left turn but the smooth flow is interrupted by a large round-about junction providing access to two medieval thorough-fares joining from the south, Maryport Street and Monday Market Street. Today the Georgian Castle Inn, looks across this busy intersection to its Tudor neighbour the White Bear in Monday Market Street.

The older pub was originally called The Talbot and retains the character of a traditional English inn,

THE TRUST FOR DEVIZES

THE WHITE BEAR
FIRST LANDLORD
RECORDED IN
1567

The cream-paint stucco façade of White Bear mask early timber fram construction.

This ancient hostelry retains the character of a traditional English inn, with wood panelled walls, timber floors and dark beams.

with wood-panelled walls, timber floors and dark beams. It's hard to get a sense of how this area would have looked when this historic hostelry was built in the 1400s. The narrow cobbled walkway of St John's Alley (a ten minute walk away) provides a visual clue.

Customers have reported seeing shadows walking behind the bar.

The White Bear, reputed to be the oldest pub in Devizes, was trading as an inn fifty years before Henry VIII was born. The earliest recorded landlord was in 1567, the same year the first lottery in England was held. Henry's daughter, the first Queen Elizabeth, introduced this initiative rather than increase taxes to raise money for ships and harbours.

A dozen years ago, landlord at the time, Bryan Smith-Dowse, invited members of Swindon-based ghost hunting group *South West Paranormal* to investigate unexplained happenings he had experienced in the pub. While Bryan was showing Billy McLeod round the pub, the ghost hunting medium became aware of a young female phantom in a 1960s' style floral dress. He was also conscious of the presence of a young man in a butcher's apron, whose name was Mark and who died in 1989 at the age of twenty-nine, having possibly taken his own life.

In the bar area, Billy had a sense of a highwayman and a young boy. He said the man was about thirty and may have been called David Robson or Robeson and gained the impression, in his former life, this phantom had been a real ladies' man. In the cellar, Billy reported sensing a young woman being pinned up against the wall by a man with a ferocious temper. The assailant, had a moustache and was about 6ft 2in. Intrigued by this reported incident the group later held a séance and came up with the name Lucy.

A spectre is thought to walk along this corridor and through the former dining room which now serves as an office.

Fiona, the present landlady, runs the pub with her husband Geoff and both have experienced things in the pub they cannot explain. Fiona said one of the housekeepers coming downstairs for some towels noticed a book on the floor in one of the rooms. When she returned with the towels the book was back on the shelf – it was the bible! One day when this staff member was on the top floor and Fiona on the first, they both heard a man's voice call out 'hello!' Both ladies thought one of the guests hadn't left but when checking they found they were quite alone.

On another occasion, when the bedrooms were being refitted, Fiona found the beds too heavy to move so, to protect the mattresses, began wrapping them in plastic sheeting using Sellotape. Part way through the task the Sellotape went missing and has never been found. During this period of disruption Fiona allowed the builders to store their tools and equipment in one of the letting rooms overnight. For security she gave them the key to the room but when they returned the following morning they discovered some of the tools had been moved to another room during the night.

Customers have reported seeing shadows moving behind the bar which coincides with feelings both Fiona and Geoff have had that a spirit wanders through the building along a former access route. The phantom walks along a passage from the direction of the gent's toilet and passes through a former dining room, now used as an office. Geoff thinks this route might have passed between earlier buildings and possibly continued ahead along a course passing under the archway of a neighbouring Tudor house. When Geoff was cashing up in the office one night the temperature dropped to freezing, giving him a feeling he was not wanted there.

The trajectory of the spectre's route takes it directly through the archway of the neighbouring house known as 'The Great Porch' which dates from 1450.

On a subsequent foul night, a guest arrived riding an expensive Harley Davison motorcycle. The pub has no car park and as there were no other guests Fiona suggested the concerned man garage his bike in a corridor just off the pavement. A problem arose the following morning when it was discovered the bike was too heavy to push up the gentle gradient back out onto the pavement. The only option was to start the powerful engine and ride the machine out. Fiona said the noise was deafening and shook the whole building. During the following week there were intensified unexplained happenings particularly in the kitchen when utensils kept going missing but were returned straightaway.

Downton
The White Horse

62 The Borough, Downton, Salisbury SP5 3LY

Tel: 01725 510408

Downton, on the Hampshire border, with the River Avon flowing through it, is home to the old White Horse Inn standing back behind the ancient market cross. The Georgian red brick façade of this historic hostelry hides a very much earlier timber-framed building used initially as a trading market for local wool growers. The wool was shipped down the Avon to the port of Christchurch from where it was exported to the continent. Much of the produce was smuggled out illegally to avoid punitive excise duties.

The Georgian red brick façade of this historic hostelry hides a very much earlier timber-framed building used initially as a trading market for local wool growers.

Around the fifteenth century there was a change of use for the building when it served as a guest house for visitors to the Bishop's Palace. By 1599 it had become an inn although there is a tantalizing reference to an unnamed inn at Downton in 1503 which might have been The White Horse. The layout of the building, since becoming an inn, has changed many times confusing resident ghosts who continue to follow established routes and routines.

Around ten years ago a paranormal group came to investigate tales of spooky happenings which included people seen waving from the windows when the pub was closed and locked, glasses flying

Clair, the landlady's sister, was taking down decorations in the function room when she heard someone behind her cough – but when she looked round there was nobody there.

The landlady Cheryl heard a female call her name when the pub was empty. On a couple of occasions her mother, who was helping with the early morning cleaning, saw an old man sitting here at table 3 with a half pint of beer.

off the shelves and two faces mysteriously appearing in the serving hatch space between the two bars.

Geoff (left), is a regular at the pub and also helps out part time behind the bar. On one occasion some ice buckets kept on the bottom shelf flew past his head.

Paul Whitburn, a former landlord, said when he first moved in his daughter would not settle, waking up in the middle of the night screaming, frightened by the presence of an old lady sitting on her bed. Paul himself witnessed the phenomena of a strange little orange ball emerging from the original stable block which now serves as a function room. He reported that the ball:

'…bounced four times along the ground before zipping back into the building. It was very weird, I remembered it glowed but didn't emit any ambient light of its own'.

In earlier times part of the outbuilding complex had served as a dairy where one of the dairymaids drowned in a vat of milk. Apparently the girl sold extra favours to gentlemen staying at the inn and during one of these encounters things went horribly wrong and she was murdered.

There are rumours of a tunnel hidden under the heavy flagstones which is thought to have been used by Royalist supporters during the English Civil War, attempting to escape when Parliamentary troops arrived to search the village. It seems likely there would have been times when skirmishes occurred in and around the pub with resultant bloodshed and fatalities.

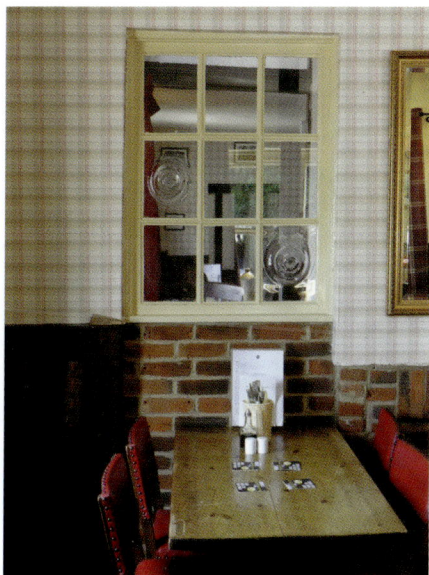

The shadow of a lady passes through this former door before turning left and disappearing through the dining room.

The buildings between the old stables and the rear entrance to the pub served as a dairy where a young woman was drowned in a vat of milk.

Malmesbury
The King's Arms Hotel
29 High Street, Malmesbury SN16 9AA

Tel: 01666 823383

www.thekahotel.co.uk

The King's Arms in Malmesbury's High Street is one of the county's oldest inns. Built in the seventeenth century a new façade was added in 1821and despite the loss of the coaching trade with the emergence of railways in the 1840s, it remained a busy meeting place for farmers on market days. The ancient hostelry appears to be visited by the ghosts of two very different men of different eras who died in the inn; one peaceably and one very violently.

Wiltshire, Gloucestershire and Somerset were important areas for providing food, clothing and munitions to both sides during the English Civil War. Malmesbury itself changed hands five times between 1642 and 1645

The King's Arms in Malmesbury's High Street is one of the county's oldest hostelries and is visited by two very different ghosts of men who died in the inn; one peaceably and one very violently.

before becoming a permanent Round-head garrison. Signs of the brutality of the war are still visible on the west side wall of Malmesbury Abbey where musket ball damage can be seen at a site where prisoners were executed.

A Cavalier courier carrying a dispatch from Bristol to Oxford stopped for the night at The King's Arms. He hid the dispatch case inside a chimney before retiring to bed. Detailed accounts of what happened next vary. One tale appeared in the form of an article published in the *Daily Mirror* on Monday 17 June 1935. It tells how an Archibald Bouchier stayed at the inn, in the bedroom above the porch and had a nightmare in which he saw the Cavalier murdered.

From the old coaching entrance the town bar is on the right and the hotel bar and dining room on the left.

Later, relaying the story to a friend he was encouraged to return to the inn where upon they found the dispatch case in the chimney. Subsequently Archibald discovered Sir Ronald Bouchier, who is thought to be the murdered Cavalier, was a distant ancestor. Another version of the story says the case, in the form of a shiny leather tube, was discovered in the 1920s by builders removing a fireplace to create the archway access between the lounge bar and dining room.

We now move forward to the nineteenth century to meet a man for whom the expression *'larger than life'* might have been coined. In 1880, Harry Jones succeeded his father as landlord of The King's Arms, eventually becoming one of the most famous innkeepers in the country. In 1908 the *North Wilts Herald* published a tribute to Harry describing him as *'a veri-table John Bull in the flesh'* and *'the embodiment of the spirit of Charles Dickens'*.

'In winter and summer, in sunshine and shadow, his features wear a perpetual smile, and he is perhaps as well-known as any man in the west of England. Old customs and well-worn methods have continued to prevail in this ancient inn... and its host would have delighted the heart of Mr Pickwick for Mr Jones is not harassed by nightmares of fashion and his house is unassailed by the artificiality of the upholsterer or the inventions of modern tawdriness.'

CCTV captured the moment when shot glasses on this shelf in the town bar flew across the room.

Harry loved having his photo taken standing outside the inn and a number of these can be seen in Malmesbury Museum confirming the description of him in this newspaper tribute:

'His portly form and jolly red face set off to perfection in the old-world habiliments which he delights to affect – trousers turned up at the ankles, a long loose fitting coat of a cut of other days, a white or brightly coloured waistcoat of the Dick Swiveller* pattern, and on his head a tall straight-brimmed hat of a style which was popular 50 or 75 years ago, and which is, in truth and in fact his crowning glory.'

*Dick Swiveller is a character from Charles Dickens' novel The Old Curiosity Shop.

Harry's gold hat is displayed in the museum along with copies of the many letters he received from famous admirers. In the early twentieth century Harry Jones died in the hotel he loved so much. Over the years staff at The King's Arms have reported odd disturbances, usually in the bar and, most strongly, in room 9 where he passed away. They put these activities down to the mischievous old former landlord, who infrequently manifests, as a portly gentleman with a wide smile.

When the current licensees Stuart and Maria took over the inn they were unaware of the ghostly history but, even after experiencing a number of paranormal happenings they accept it with good humour. Furnishings in the lounge bar include two solidly-built round-top tables each displaying a small glass flower vase. Often, when no one else is around, one of the vases slides to the edge of the table and drops vertically without spilling the water or breaking the glass. This happens so regularly the nonplussed proprietors simply pick them up and replace them.

Harry Jones, seen here wearing his famous gold hat, died in room 9 of The King's Arms but continues to mischievously revisit from time to time. (Courtesy of Malmesbury Museum.)

The town bar is in a separate room across the other side of the coaching entry. An incident here was captured on CCTV when shot glasses on a high level shelf inexplicably flew across the room.

Stuart and Maria, the current licensees have experienced a number of paranormal happenings at the pub including the vase on this table regularly dropping vertically to the floor.

Malmesbury
The Old Bell Hotel

Abbey Row, Malmesbury SN16 0BW

Tel: 01666 822344

www.oldbellhotel.co.uk

The Old Bell at Malmesbury has one of the richest histories of any of Wiltshire's inns. When you look into its past it's not surprising the ancient hostelry has a few secrets and has built up quite a haunted reputation. The east wing experiences most of the paranormal activity which is unsurprising when you learn it was built on part of the abbey churchyard and eight stone sarcophagi were discovered in a vaulted cellar extending

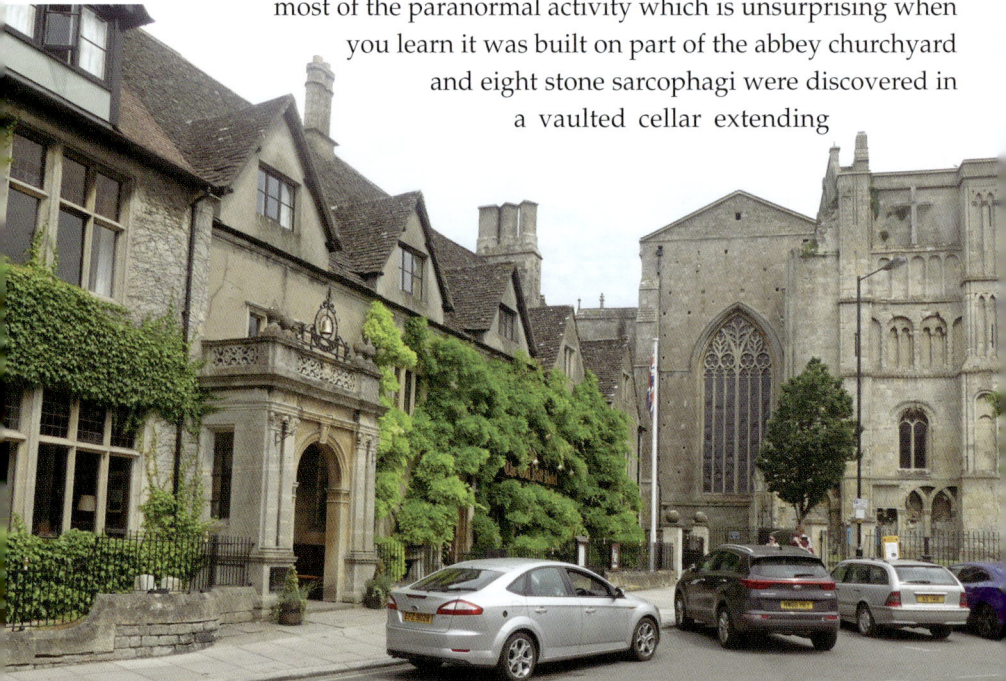

The Old Bell and Malmesbury Abbey have been the closest of neighbours for 800 yea

beneath the lounge and bar. Night staff report hearing odd sounds and feeling cold spots particularly near the saloon bar during their nightly rounds. Some are convinced they were being followed.

Around the year 1130, the Bishop of Salisbury built a castle west of Malmesbury Abbey, designed in part it seems, to upset the monks. During the civil wars between King Stephen and Empress Matilda the castle changed hands several times but, despite its defences being strengthened in 1173-4, was abandoned soon afterwards. In 1216 the monks were given permission to demolish it and Abbot Loring built a guest house on the site, using materials from the old castle keep.

The east wing was built on part of the abbey churchyard and eight stone sarcophagi were discovered in a vaulted cellar extending beneath the lounge and bar.

When the abbey was dissolved under Henry VIII in the sixteenth century, the guest house became a cloth mill. By 1603, however, it had become an inn. Originally known as The Castle, it was renamed The Bell by the end of the eighteenth century.

The door to Athelstan room faces the enigmatic portrait of the Grey Lady across the landing.

The ghost of the unknown lady in the portrait on the staircase floats through the hotel.

Spooky goings-on have occurred in the Danvers Room, Foe Room and the James Ody room. When I visited, a guest, unaware of the hotel's haunted reputation, was requesting at reception to be moved from Athelstan because she felt an uneasy presence. Frightened guests in the Danvers Room have reported belongings being thrown across the bedroom by unseen hands. Bed sheets were also pulled in the middle of the night by an unknown entity.

One of the most baffling incidents took place outside and inside The Foe Room. Returning residents were surprised when they were unable to gain access. Although the door could be unlocked, it could only be opened a fraction. Staff were called but they too failed to budge the door. With no other course of action left, a ladder was fetched and propped up outside and beneath the bedroom window. A member of staff climbed the ladder up to the window, which was securely fastened, the only way in was to smash the glass. Once inside, the staff member was stunned to see that a heavy wooden wardrobe had been manoeuvred against the door despite the room being empty.

One of the most commonly reported sightings is of the 'Grey Lady', who is often seen in the James Ody room by residents and staff alike. She is described as looking forlorn and melancholy as she glides silently around the hotel. Hanging on the staircase, is a portrait of a woman wearing a long black mourning dress. This has led to speculation that the figure in the painting could be the grey lady whose identity remains a mystery. Some say she was the victim of an unhappy and forced marriage which took place at the abbey but why this should cause her to haunt the hotel is not explained. Why her portrait (if it is the same woman) should hang in the hotel is another unknown.

In addition to its rich heritage The Old Bell is one of the best appointed hotels in the country, retaining many of its original features. The hotel staff are more than happy to accommodate ghost hunters and paranormal researchers, should you decide to undertake your own investigation.

The Grey Lady, seen by residents and staff alike, often makes an appearance here in the James Ody room.

Melksham
The King's Arms

20 Market Place, Melksham SN12 6EX

Tel: 01225 707272

www.kingsarmsmelksham.co.uk

Published in 1792, Archibald Robertson's *Typographical Survey of the Great Road from London to Bath and Bristol* informs us that:

> '*Melksham is a small neat town, ninety six miles from London, pleasantly situated on the banks of the lower Avon, on which stand several cloth and corn mills. The houses are in general good, partly built of stone, and partly of brick; and a handsome house and pleasure-ground, belonging to the Thresher family, is situated close to the town on the left.*'

As many as ten stagecoaches a day clattered over the old cobbled forecourt of the eighteenth-century King's Arms where the colourful tables are set out today.

Situated in the bustling market place the eighteenth-century King's Arms was Melksham's principal coaching inn with as many as ten coaches a day stopping for refreshment and a change of horses. Consequently the ancient hostelry is steeped in history and not surprisingly associated with tales

of notorious highwaymen. The low building on the left of the main photograph is the original stables now transformed into a restaurant.

Today the benign apparition of a little girl manifests here. One startled witness said she appeared dripping wet in a bedroom and: *'looked like a black and white photograph'*. The girl's identity has not been established but her wet-through state suggests she may have caught a chill after being out in a downpour or possibly drowned in the River Avon. A plaque on the current town bridge informs us that it replaced a former structure which collapsed in 1809 in a storm, which we can conclude must have been very violent.

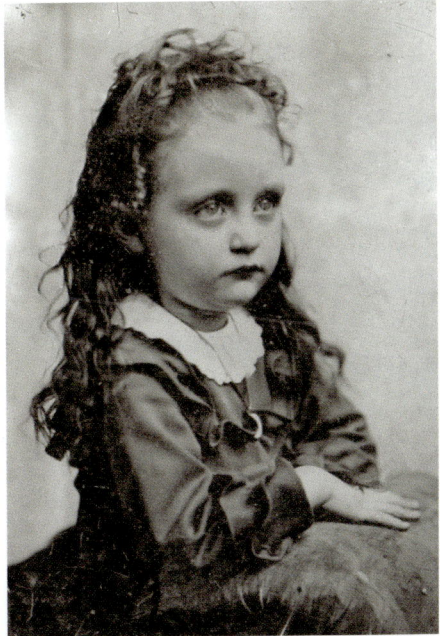

The apparition of a little girl in Victorian dress appears in different locations in the hotel.

In 1809 a violent storm swept away the former bridge over the River Avon.

'Max' the mysterious apparition appears sitting in front of the statue in the corner before the pub opens for business.

Naomi, a present member of staff, recently saw the little girl in the cellar, sitting on the steps. This suggests the child might have been familiar with the building and possibly the daughter of someone connected with the inn in Victorian times rather than the daughter of one of the guests. One of the housekeeping staff has also seen the little girl sitting by a window in one of the rooms. In the corner of the lounge is an alcove containing a statue. The apparition of a man, who the staff call Max, appears regularly sitting on the bench seat in front of the alcove.

The Lower Avon, seen from the town bridge, where there have been a number of deaths by drowning over the years.

Monkton Farleigh
The King's Arms

42 Monkton Farleigh, Bradford-on-Avon BA15 2QH

Tel: 01225 859761

www.thekingsarmsmf.com

This beautiful seventeenth-century inn has a courtyard in front and a large rear garden with far reaching views over open countryside. Inside is a spacious L-shaped room for drinking and dining. The inn is said to have been built on the site of an eleventh-century Cluniac priory. Reports claim it to be haunted by the ghost of an elderly medieval monk and a distressed Victorian lady.

The oldest part of the inn was possibly built by the monks in 1090 more or less as an estate office where they could officiate and administer the affairs of their Farleigh property. One of the friars was found dead slumped over his desk in what is now the bar. His

This beautiful seventeenth-century inn has a courtyard at the front and a large rear garden with far reaching views over open country-side.

The oldest part of the inn was possibly built by monks in 1090 as place to administer the affairs of their Farleigh property. One of the friars was found dead slumped over his desk in what is now the bar.

death was sudden and unexplained and his spirit continues to pervade the inn and local vicinity. His hooded figure has been spotted walking slowly from the pub to the Monk's Conduit (water source) via the Manor where he passes through a door and disappears.

Referred to as 'The Black Monk', the departed cleric has a wicked sense of humour playing tricks on both residents and staff. Much of the unwanted activity includes spiriting away important items of dress or work tools and switching lights on and off. People have also reported hearing the sound of muffled laughter.

Very experienced chef Lewis Davies and his wife Charlotte took over as licensees in April 2018 and soon became aware of frequent odd disturbances.

Lewis and Charlotte Davies took over as licensees at The King's Arms in April 2018 and soon became aware of frequent odd disturbances. One night Lewis got out of bed to investigate the sound of footsteps along the corridor leading from their bedroom thinking it might be burglars. At that time he was unaware a number of previous licensees had reported they often heard heavy footsteps clumping up the stairs and walking the length of the upper floor.

Charlotte says a toilet roll is moved off a holder in one of the guest bathrooms and placed in the middle of the bedroom floor. She also says she sets the dining room tables as her last job of the day but in the morning one of the place settings is disturbed with the fork being laid across the knife to form a cross.

Some nights the fork on this single place setting is unaccountably moved to lay across the knife.

Eric Muspratt, a landlord during the 1980s, reported several unexplained incidents including a creaking door downstairs followed by stomping footsteps up the stairs and along the passage. He said one morning at 1.30 a freezer being defrosted in the room above the bar suddenly tilted over sending a stream of water through the ceiling. Charlotte, unaware of the freezer incident, suffered a similar disaster after choosing the same spot to have her washing machine plumbed in.

A box containing a strange key was found when this inglenook fire-place was revealed during renovation work in the 1990s.

Eric Muspratt, a landlord from the 1980s, reported hearing this door creak at night after the pub was locked and bolted.

Far right: A former landlady who failed to heed warnings about renovation work from two mysterious men fell on these stairs and injured her neck.

During the Victorian era, a local lady was driving her carriage home late one night when her horse took fright and bolted. The terrified woman desperately tried to regain control but her gig clipped the inn wall overturning the vehicle and fatally injuring her. She was carried into the inn but it was soon discovered the services of a priest were required rather than those of a doctor. Although her phantom has rarely been seen, a woman's ghostly cries have often been heard echoing throughout the building.

During internal renovation work in the 1990s two mysterious men called at the inn warning the landlady: *'no good will come of your work here'*. Having issued their warning, the two gentlemen abruptly disappeared leaving the woman somewhat shocked and stunned. Regardless of the threat, renovations continued revealing a huge inglenook fireplace with a double-skinned back wall. A box was found inside the cavity containing a strange key. The key was inserted in every lock in the building but failed to fit any of them.

This tantalizing artifact is still part of the pub property and Lewis has hopes of resolving the mystery.

Eccentric and delightful in equal parts, the Haunch of Venison was built in 1320 as a church house for the adjacent St Thomas's church.

Salisbury
Haunch of Venison
1 Minster Street, Salisbury SP1 1TB
Tel: 01722 411313

Eccentric and delightful in equal parts, the Haunch of Venison was built in 1320 as a church house for the adjacent St Thomas's church and accommodated men working on the Cathedral's spire. The three small bars known locally as 'the Horsebox', 'Death Row' and, at the top, 'House of Lords' were once frequented by the master masons. This ancient hostelry was later used as a brothel and a tunnel linking the pub to St Thomas's church was excavated so clergymen could visit without embarrassment.

Recorded as an inn from the sixteenth century, it was one of the original chop houses. These 'men only' quality establishments were renowned for hearty eating and good company, where businessmen gathered to hatch deals over plates of traditionally cooked meats washed down with fine wines and good ales.

Interesting and historical features include a pewter-topped bar and rows of taps which at one time were used to dispense spirits and fortified wines.

Two unrelated ghosts are said to haunt the premises. The first derives from a phenomenon known as 'The Hand of Glory'. This is the dried and pickled hand of a man who has been hanged for murder. Medieval beliefs attribute great powers to a Hand of Glory combined with a candle made of fat from the corpse of the same malefactor. The lighted candle placed

in the Hand of Glory, was said to render motionless all persons to whom it was presented.

In 1903 the pickled hand of a man was discovered under floorboards by builders working at the pub. An enterprising landlord displayed the gruesome artefact holding a fan of playing cards. It was preserved for years in a glass case in the bar and gave rise to the legend of 'The Demented Whist Player' involving a stranger arriving on the Southampton coach one evening in the 1820s seeking food and lodgings. In classic hustler mode he bought drinks for some locals playing cards and was invited to join them. He lost quite heavily at first encouraging other players to up the stakes. Alcohol flowed freely and the stranger's 'win some, lose some' luck improved until he was substantially ahead of the game. A drunken young butcher who had lost far more than he could afford took exception and accused the newcomer of cheating. As things became really heated the butcher drew a blade and with a single expert chop severed the man's hand at the wrist. As it fell to the floor it was seen to be holding five aces.

The old bread oven – inset on the left hand side of the inglenook fireplace – is used today to display the pickled hand of a man said to have been caught cheating at cards.

It may be presumed the man died from shock or loss of blood or both and his ghost is now responsible for phantom footfalls heard late at night. Equally it might really be the actions of the felon who was hanged for murder and whose hand has been preserved as a gruesome spectacle. The ghost, whoever he might be, is accused of hiding objects, moving glasses across tables, opening and closing doors and switching electrical appliances on and off.

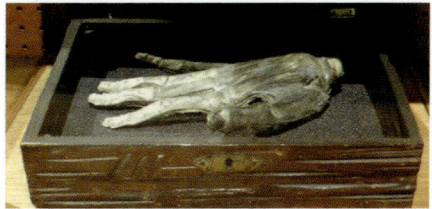

A Hand of Glory on display at Whitby Museum.

The haunted stairs where many people have detected the strange aroma of freshly turned earth and grass.

In 2010 the Haunch of Venison made international headlines when the hand was stolen. Following the ensuing publicity the gruesome artefact was returned in a bubble wrap envelope courtesy of Royal Mail. Justine Millar, Manager at the time, said we were expecting delivery of a beer tap and the poor girl that opened it screamed: '*Oh my God, The hand!*' Today the legendary relic is housed more securely behind a grill in the former inglenook bread oven.

The second ghost pervading this ancient inn is the 'Grey Lady', an old woman wearing a shawl who appears at windows. She manifests from time to time on the stairs in the pub unaccountably leaving behind an aroma of freshly tilled earth and grass. She is also seen outside the Haunch of Venison, particularly in the narrow alleyway between the pub and St Thomas's church. It is said she lived near The Poultry Cross during the late Victorian era and one evening sent her young son to buy drink from the pub. The lad didn't return and was never seen again and the mother seems doomed to an eternal quest of searching for him.

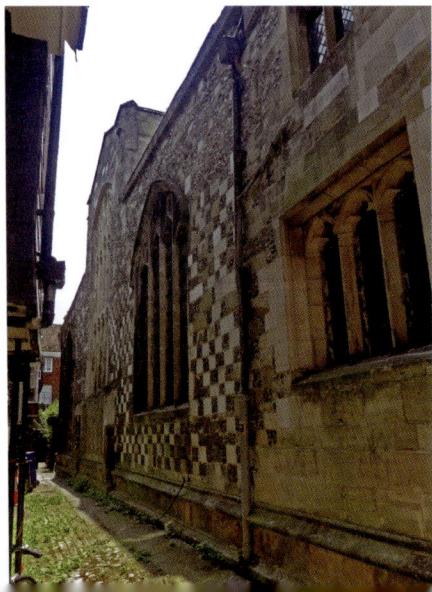

The alleyway between the Haunch of Venison and St Thomas's church where the Grey Lady has been seen.

Salisbury
The Rai d'Or

69 Brown Street, Salisbury SP1 2AS

Tel: 01722 327137

www.raidor.co.uk

The Rai d'Or was built in the sixteenth century as a reconstruction of the original thirteenth-century tavern. As with so many buildings in and around the city its early purpose was to accommodate workmen engaged in building Salisbury Cathedral.

The Rai d'Or (or Rydedorre) on the corner of Trinity and Brown Street was once known as The Star. It has recently reverted to the name it went by in the Middle Ages. The present building was constructed in the sixteenth century as a reconstruction of the original thirteenth-century tavern. As with so many buildings in and around the city its early purpose was to accommodate workmen engaged in building Salisbury Cathedral. Over the years this ancient pub is said to be home to five friendly ghosts. Today The Rai d'Or functions successfully as a combined Thai restaurant and free house.

This ancient pub is said to be home to five friendly ghosts, one of whom known as 'The Doctor', can sometimes be seen standing by the inglenook fire-place.

SALISBURY CIVIC SOCIETY

Here dwelt

Agnes Bottenham

Landlady of the Rydedorre
who founded
Trinity Hospital
for the poor
circa 1370

Agnes Bottenham, Salisbury's best known 'madam', was intent on looking after her girls in their retirement.

In the thirteenth century nearby 'Love Lane' was at the centre of the red light district and Agnes Bottenham, the tavern's most famous host, ran a brothel from the premises. In 1998 a tunnel was discovered under the bar of The Rai d'Or leading from the back of the building in the direction of the Cathedral. Perhaps, as with the Haunch of Venison, this subterranean access provided a route for clergymen entering the premises without being seen.

The original building had an external double staircase with a balcony where the working girls displayed their charms. One of the five resident ghosts known as 'The Doctor' can some-times be seen standing in the vicinity of the inglenook fire-place. In 1370, as penance for her involvement in the whoring business, Agnes gifted land in Trinity Street (behind the tavern) for the foundation of Trinity Hospital as a sanctuary for retired prostitutes. Rebuilt in 1705 as almshouses and modernized in 1998, The Trinity Hospital now provides retire-ment housing for 22 Salisbury residents in single bedroom flats. A recent report from a visiting relative described the situation:

Rebuilt in 1705 as almshouses and modernized in 1998, The Trinity Hospital now provides retirement housing for 22 Salisbury residents in well-appointed single bedroom flats.

'I've just spent three days with my 90-year old aunt, who has a delightful, bright, spacious one-bedroomed flat on the first floor, which she accesses by lift. She is happily settled and is well supported by the excellent and obviously caring Warden. The gardens are lovely and well kept, and provide an outdoor communal space which I saw was well used, as, Auntie told me, is the large and bright communal lounge.'

The Trinity Hospital Courtyard Chapel, open daily from 9 am until 5 pm, offers a quiet refuge from the bustle of the busy city.

Salisbury
The Red Lion Hotel

Milford Street, Salisbury SP1 2AN

Tel: 01722 323334

www.the-redlion.co.uk

The classical Georgian façade of The Red Lion in Milford Street belies the thirteenth-century origins of one of the finest examples of a coaching inn in the country. A different, almost magical world, greets visitors as they pass through the huge coaching arch into the medieval cobbled courtyard, richly decorated with flowers, shrubs and an impressive hanging creeper believed to be the oldest in Europe.

The hotel's interior continues to delight with its fine collection of antiques, especially the many clocks, including 'Parliament clocks' and in particular, the Skeleton and Organ Clock in reception whose case was carved by prisoners of war captured following defeat of the Spanish Armada.

In 2014, Best Western purchased The Red Lion from the Maidment family who had owned and run the hotel for the previ-

The classical Georgian façade of The Red Lion in Milford Street belies the thirteenth-century origins of one of the finest examples of a coaching inn in the country.

The medieval courtyard is richly decorated with flowers, shrubs and a hanging creeper believed to be Europe's oldest.

ous eighty years. Molly Maidment, born at the inn and associated with it during all that time, wrote a memoir of her early life spent here. In her biography, *Child of The Red Lion*, she confesses to have been horrified and mesmerised by the slithering eels kept in tanks under the garage floor and further confides:

'I suffered from another source of persistent nightmares. A porter was found with his throat slashed and took several agonizing days to die. All the gruesome details of the porter's suicide were graphically recounted to me over and over again by an hysterical chambermaid.'

Laura has witnessed paranormal happenings in the 1220 bar, the oldest part of the hotel.

It is tempting to think this might be the source of the poltergeist activity experienced in the 1220 bar, the oldest part of the hotel. Laura, who works on reception and helps out in the bar, says there is a particular spot in the room which is subject to a mysterious force. A cleaning notice warning of a slippery floor was placed here and captured on CCTV flying across the room. On another occasion one of Laura's colleagues passed over the spot carrying a tray of drinks when one of the glasses smashed for no apparent reason. In her book, Molly raised the question of ghosts:

'As with so many old hotels, there are recurrent rumours of ghostly sightings and as a child I was much too scared to go alone in the evenings along one medieval passage. In this corridor, with its sloping, creaking floors, I occasionally sensed that unseen people were processing to and fro. I never actually saw a ghost but to this day there have been reports of ghostly sightings, or more accurately ghostly footsteps.'

Left: A cleaning notice warning of a slippery floor was placed here and captured on CCTV flying across the room.

Above: Rooms 17 and 29 in the oldest wing of the hotel are noted for reports of eerie feelings and a potential for paranormal activity.

Of the 51 rooms in the hotel three in particular, 17, 29 and 'The Seamstress Suite' are noted for reports of eerie feelings and a potential for paranormal activity. They are situated in the southern medieval wing built between 1280 and 1320 as a hostel for the draughtsmen constructing the Cathedral.

Today The Seamstress Suite, is all luxury and comfort. Beautifully appointed with classic-contemporary décor it even has a free standing cast iron tub at the centre in addition to a walk-in shower with spa toiletries. However, in earlier times, this was the cramped living and poorly-lit work space for a team of women and girls responsible for the hotel's soft furnishings and sewing requirements.

The ghost of one of these lowly workers, who would never have seen a private bathroom, let alone one with spa toiletries, might be responsible for the sound of weeping reported when the room is unoccupied. Perhaps she was the victim of an all too common occurrence of those times when a girl was sacked from her job for becoming pregnant out of wedlock. Too frightened to go home and confess to their parents, and with no prospect of earning money outside of prostitution, they could see no future. In her book, Molly mentions just such a scenario involving one of the hotel chambermaids.

Another recent unexplained happening occurred when a guest whose room overlooked the courtyard made enquiries at reception about the party he had seen the previous night with people dressed in Tudor costume. Both he and the receptionist were bemused to discover there was no such party.

Today The Seamstress Suite, is all luxury and comfort but in earlier times it was the cramped living and poorly-lit work space for a team of women.

The case of the Skeleton and Organ Clock in reception was carved by prisoners of war following defeat of the Spanish Armada.

Salisbury
The Wig and Quill
1 New Street, Salisbury SP1 2PH

Tel: 01722 335665

www.thewigandquill.com

The Wig and Quill fronting New Street was built in 1594.

The foundation stones of Salisbury Cathedral were laid on 28 April 1220 following the clergy's decision to move their administrative centre 2 miles from Old Sarum. As New Sarum (Salisbury) developed around the great church the first established road was simply referred to as New Street, and a section of it still is. This medieval thoroughfare extends in a long straight line from a river crossing at its western end (now Crane Bridge) to the village of St Martins in the east.

When the roadside hostelry, now known as The Wig and Quill, was built in 1594, England and its queen were in somewhat of a decline. The Spanish Armada had been defeated six

Long standing staff member Julie has felt something poke her in the back when walking through the kitchen door into the bar.

years earlier but in the 1590s Elizabeth I was worn-out and a little of the gloss had come off her reputation and achievements. Unemployment and taxation were both high, harvests failed in 1594–7, and hard times led to rising crime rates and record numbers of executions.

Despite this unpromising background there was money and optimism enough to press ahead with building a new inn. Today The Wig and Quill is seen as a traditional English pub with one long bar divided into three drinking areas. There are standing timbers, oak beams overhead and large open fires to provide warmth in winter. It also has a pleasant courtyard and a secluded, walled garden which is very colourful in summer.

The chef has reported seeing the ghost of a little girl standing inside the front entrance by this ancient upright timber.

As you might expect, in an establishment that has been trading for well over 400 years, this ancient pub has its share of ghost stories. Julie, who has worked here for four years said a number of the staff have experienced paranormal happenings. On several occasions Julie has felt something poke her in the back as she passed through the kitchen doorway into the bar. She also said that a temporary barmaid working in her summer break from university saw glasses fly off the shelf above the bar. The chef has seen the ghost of a little girl standing near the entrance by the ancient upright timber. Perhaps she ventured into the pub or was she waiting to go out and play? It is tempting to think she (and perhaps other naughty ghostly children) are responsible for unexplained happenings in a neighbouring house.

In Frogg Moody and Richard Nash's book *Haunted Salisbury*, the authors tell the story of the house when it was occupied by Jim and Pearl Shergold. The couple's baby, whilst sitting

As you might expect an establishment that has been trading for well over 400 years has its share of ghost stories.

The one long bar is divided into three drinking areas with oak beams overhead and large open fires providing warmth in the winter.

The rear dining room opens onto a secluded, walled garden which is very colourful in summer.

in her high chair, acted as though she could see someone or something – invisible to others – moving around the room and at 6 p.m. every evening the Shergolds were disturbed by their doorbell ringing. The bell was operated by an old fashioned pull handle connected to a wire which rang an internal bell on a spring.

The Shergolds blamed the nuisance on naughty children and one evening Jim lay in wait by the front door. Sure enough the bell rang at 6 p.m. but when he raced out the street was empty. The couple were renting the house from the City Council and when they complained about the bell ringing and other occurrences they were told previous tenants had moved out because of the strange goings on.

Wanborough
The Harrow Inn

High Street, Wanborough, Swindon SN4 0AE

Tel: 01793 791792

www.theharrowinnwanborough.co.uk

The Grade II Harrow Inn on Wanborough High Street is a quintessential, thatched English pub. Parts of the building date back to 1747 when it was known as The Harrow and Kings Head. It started life as a coaching inn and is said to be haunted by at least 10 ghosts including that of 'Old Marley', a coachman who overturned his vehicle outside the inn killing himself and his passengers. A number of witnesses have reported seeing Marley's ghostly apparition walking into the inn and also appearing in the dining room. The popular theory is he wanders the building at night looking for his missing passengers.

This quintessential, thatched English pub started life as a coaching inn in 1747.

Landlady Michelle has frequently been aware of a mysterious presence in the pub.

Former landlord David Gray recalled a French family visiting Wiltshire to see crop circles who called in to the Harrow for lunch. Having been told the pub was haunted the Frenchman pulled out of his pocket something resembling a plumb bob. Holding it above his hand it rotated in such a way to suggest the pub had not one, but 10 ghosts.

When David was landlord his bedroom was directly below an attic room which was sealed off with a heavy wardrobe placed in front of the door because it had no ceiling and was still exposed to the thatch. David reported hearing heavy footsteps walking backwards and forwards in the loft. When his daughter returned from University and slept in the room next door to the sealed room, she woke very hot one night and pushed down the duvet. Then becoming really cold tried to pull the cover up again but she was unable to move. She said it was as if her arms were pinned down and she could feel pressure on top of her.

The former inn stables have been converted into self-catering units with one named after Old Marley, the phantom coachman.

Subsequent landlord Andrew Ridler, reported many strange happenings thought to be the work of 'a host of ghosts'. One customer watched as a bottle of coke moved forward on a shelf and without tilting dropped vertically onto the floor. One of the bar staff saw a candle on a dining room table flare up and fly across the room. Current barmaid Tracey and landlady Michelle, looked on in amazement as one of the balloons they were preparing for a party started moving vertically and horizontally about the bar in a bizarre and erratic way the string at all times hanging straight down.

Chef Ian confirms the quantity of spirits who make their presence felt in and around the kitchen. One of them is a tall bearded man but many are children. Ian is not a practising medium but has been sensitive to the presence of ghosts all his life and on occasion is able to communicate with them. He says a little girl called Stephanie appears near the fireplace in the bar, she is around ten years old and wears a floral dress. A young boy named Charlie also appears near the fireplace and makes the kettle swing. He passes two spirits so regularly along a corridor on the second floor he says good morning to them.

Chef Ian confirms there are at least 10 ghosts with a lot of paranormal activity in and around the kitchen and by the fire in the bar.

A kettle hanging in the fireplace is made to swing by the ghost of a little boy named Charlie.

Selected Bibliography

Haunted Places of Wiltshire, Rupert Matthews

Haunted Salisbury, Frogg Moody and Richard Nash

Haunted Wiltshire, Keith Wills

Paranormal Wiltshire, David Scanlan

The Haunted Pub Guide, Guy Lyon Playfair

The Inns of Wiltshire, Andrew Swift and Kirsten Elliott

Wiltshire Ghost Stories, Richard Holland

Plus three very useful websites:

    hauntedplaces.org

    ghostpubs.com

    eerieplace.com

The east wing of The Old Bell at Malmesbury experiences most of the paranormal activity which is unsurprising when you learn it was built on part of the abbey church-yard and eight stone sarcophagi were discovered in a vaulted cellar extending beneath the lounge and bar.